Lady G

A Biography of
The Honourable Lady Goulding LL D

Lady G

A Biography of
The Honourable Lady Goulding LL D

Jacqueline Hayden

TOWN HOUSE

Published in 1994 by
Town House and Country House
Trinity House
Charleston Road
Ranelagh, Dublin 6
Ireland

A CIP catalogue record for this book is available from the British Library

ISBN: 0-948524-70-7

The photographs in this book are from the personal collection of Lady Valerie Goulding.

Cover photograph: The Honourable Lady Goulding LL D, photographed by Sir Geoffrey Shackerley

Cover design: Bill Murphy
Typeset by Typeform Ltd
Printed in Ireland by ßetaprint

For a friend . . . for Frank

Acknowledgements

It is no easy thing to write a biography of a living person. My task would have been impossible without the cooperation and support of Lady Valerie Goulding and her sons. I am most grateful to the Goulding family for all their comment and opinion. I am indebted to everyone quoted in the text for their time and help. Many of those who helped in my researches prefer to remain anonymous, but they too deserve my gratitude.

I should like in particular to acknowledge the help of Dr James White and Bobbie Ballagh, who took me on an expert tour of modern Irish art for the chapter on Sir Basil Goulding. Máirín Byrne provided an excellent historical overview of the treatment and services available for disabled persons in Ireland between the 1950s and now. Ken Holden gave me a considered assessment of Lady Valerie's contribution to the development of the CRC. Geraldine Cruess-Callaghan was a reliable sounding board where opinions differed and was most generous with her time and memories. Dr A J F O'Reilly brought me on an amusing, sagacious and stimulating romp through his views on Lady Valerie's psyche.

I am very grateful to Mike Murphy, who introduced me to Lady Valerie, for his conviction that I was the right person to undertake the task of writing her biography.

CONTENTS

1   Monckton's daughter   1

2   A window on the eye of the storm   22

3   Having a jolly good time   40

4   Doing her bit   75

5   The Central Remedial Clinic   86

6   Life at Dargle Cottage   119

7   Willie B   140

8   A soldier of destiny   186

9   Uncomfortable transitions   198

1

MONCKTON'S DAUGHTER

Valerie comes from the best of both strands within the Anglo-Irish tradition. Though she's not an intellectual she has marked her passage through life by real achievement and Irish society is better because of her. I think of her as a benign activist; she's part Thatcher, part Florence Nightingale and part sergeant-major.

Dr A J F O'Reilly's assessment of Valerie Goulding encompasses most, if not all, of the characteristics that have made her the woman she is. She likes to say that she is more Irish than the Irish themselves, but her values and background are quintessentially English. She was born near her grandfather's Tudor manor house in Kent just before the end of the First World War, and her childhood world was dominated by war, duty, hierarchical class structures and by a social life that centred around horses and dogs. Although she was only twenty years of age when she first came to Ireland on a spree with her brother Gilbert, Valerie was already a woman who was comfortable in the company of statesmen and royalty.

This ease and familiarity with her 'betters' must have made Valerie appear quite an exotic creature when she attended Fairyhouse Races in the spring of 1939. Although nine years her senior, Sir Basil Goulding was much impressed by the young Englishwoman he met in the company of his Trinity College pals, and he cajoled Valerie into extending her short weekend break from the War Office, where she was then working. Before the end of the summer, just days before the outbreak of the war, Valerie and Basil were married. After the war they settled in Ireland, but it was not long before Valerie began looking for 'something to do': that 'something' eventually became the Central

Remedial Clinic, a pioneering and world-renowned centre catering for handicapped children. The initial impetus, however, was Valerie's reaction to the polio epidemics that swept Ireland in the 1940s and 1950s. When Dr O'Reilly speaks of the Irish strand of the Anglo-Irish tradition, he is talking about Valerie's ability to communicate and empathise with people: when he speaks about the English strand he is talking about her sense of *noblesse oblige* and her conviction, as he puts it, that 'she must be about God's business'. Characteristically, in both elements of Valerie Goulding's personality the influence of her beloved father is uppermost.

Valerie's abiding memory of her father's advice was that she must 'do something' in life and that she must work. Nowadays Walter Monckton would be called a 'workaholic'. A king's counsel who was incapable of leaving his briefs at home when he went on holiday, Walter played a key role as friend and adviser to Edward VIII at the time of the abdication crisis in 1936. During World War II he was, for a time, director of the Ministry of Information. He later ran for Parliament on the advice and urging of Sir Winston Churchill, and was minister of defence at the beginning of the Suez crisis. Clearly it was from her father that Valerie acquired her sometimes manic energy or constant 'activism', as one close friend describes it. The Thatcher-like qualities are there in Walter's personality as well: the will to succeed and the determination not to be thwarted are all part of Valerie's panoply of inherited absolutes.

Valerie once described herself, somewhat disingenuously, as having always been 'someone's daughter, wife or mother'. Whatever about the latter two, she is most definitely her father's daughter. A writer could be accused of stating the obvious in pointing out the importance of childhood influences in moulding the future adult. In Valerie's case there is no doubt that her relationship with her father and his unsuccessful relationship with Valerie's mother, Polly, were key factors in forming her personality:

> As Walter is leaving me this term I feel that I must write a few lines to tell you how sorry I am to lose him. To me personally he has been of the greatest assistance in the house, and his influence in the school generally has been considerable and has always been used in the right direction. It has been a

great comfort to me to have such a trustworthy boy to help me. I feel sure that you will be satisfied with him and that he is certain to get on well in whatever position he may be placed.

I hope he will often come to Harrow after he has left; he has many friends here and I shall be always glad to see him and to put him up, if he can stay.

With kind regards to Mrs Monckton,

Yours sincerely,

J C Moss[1]

Walter's father, Frank, frequently received glowing reports about the performance of his son. When Walter was eight and attending a preparatory school, The Knoll, Woburn Sands, his headmaster E F M Miller wrote: 'I must write a line to say how very pleased we are with your little boy. He is a capital little fellow, and I venture to predict that he will do us credit some day.'[2]

On another occasion Walter's school report noted that 'he takes the greatest pains possible'.[3] It is clear that the young Walter Monckton was a well-liked boy and a boy from whom much was expected. In 'taking the greatest pains' it is also clear that Walter, from the outset of his life, set his own standard of achievement and worked hard to fulfil his ambitions.

Both Walter's father and grandfather were local Kent worthies. His grandfather, also named Walter, had at one time been president of the Wrotham and District Conservative Association. He had also served as a Poor Law Guardian and as a magistrate. His son Frank, though less active, was a pillar of the local Kent establishment. The family had owned a paper-making business for several generations, but by the time young Walter was on the receiving end of his master's glowing reports, that industry had diminished and Frank Monckton's business largely revolved around his chairmanship of the Basted Mill near Borough Green in Kent.

Lord Birkenhead's biography of Walter Monckton depicts an idyllic childhood:

Reed House, Plaxtol, lay four miles off the Tonbridge road to Ightham, and it was here that Walter Monckton was born on 17 January 1891, and spent the first nine years of his childhood with his sister Dora, known as Dolly and two years younger than he, and his brother Leslie, who was five years younger. It was a pretty mid-Victorian house built in grey brick, with a stone porch and tower, surrounded by yews and laurels; a house of moderate size, with six or seven bedrooms, counting attics, and a billiard room, a place of chaotic disorder used for general recreation by Walter and his friends . . . .

The garden at Reed House was small and, for children, full of secret, hidden places. A fine holly tree and a beech stood outside the house, and the garden ran downhill on one side to an orchard and a lane, beyond which flowed the Bourne, a small tributary stream of the Medway. On the left was a shrubbery concealing a kitchen garden. The orchard belonged to an old man called Mr Love, adored by the children, and they had free access to it, eating as many of his apples as they liked, although Leslie was inclined to chew up his and feed them to the pigs.

On the right of the garden a footpath led down to the road below, and on the main Plaxtol road behind the house was an inn and a farm presided over by another friend, the farmer, Mr Beadle. And there was an old cobbler with a beard called Mr Rogers, whose shop near Plaxtol church, Walter and Dolly were allowed to visit as a reward for good behaviour.

In these surroundings the Monckton children grew up. There were no other buildings near Reed House and about it was the profound stillness of the countryside, broken only by the sounds of the village, the hammer on the anvil at the forge, or one of Mr Beadle's farm carts creaking into his yard.[4]

Birkenhead's prose brings to mind a Turner or Constable painting of a serene and ordered 'Little England'. Later on, he notes the excellent relationship between the Monckton family and their nanny, maid, butler, groom, cowman and gardener. Although this arcadian world escaped the physical ravages of World War I, its peace was shaken by the loss of so many of its sons. But on the surface, at least, the Kent countryside into which Valerie was born differed little from Walter's childhood surroundings.

For all its halcyon qualities, Walter's Kent was a narrow world where young men often married a childhood playmate before either had ventured into the wider world. Two years after he had gone up to Balliol College, Oxford, Walter announced that he had become engaged to Mary Adelaide Soames Colyer-Fergusson, a childhood friend who lived at Ightham Mote, very close to his own home at Ightham Warren. Known to all her friends and family as Polly, Walter's fiancée was the eldest daughter of Sir Thomas Colyer-Fergusson, heir to a Scotch baronetcy. Walter's college friends tried to dissuade him from the marriage, arguing that, having had no other relationships, he knew nothing about women. Polly and Walter ignored their advice and were married at Ightham Church on 18 July 1914 with five hundred guests in attendance. From the wedding pictures it is obvious that Polly was a striking girl with deep-set eyes and a sculptured face. But beneath the wreath of orange blossom and white heather lurked a seriousness and depth that would later cause irreconcilable friction between herself and the more garrulous Walter. So while Polly and Walter came from within miles of each other and shared many mutual friends, their apparent similarity was only skin deep.

Polly's mother had died in her thirties, leaving Sir Thomas with six young children. It was Polly who bore the brunt of rearing her younger brothers and sisters, a fact that Valerie feels affected her mother deeply. There was always a governess at Ightham Mote in the eleven or so years between the death of Sir Thomas's first wife Beatrice and his second marriage, but it was Polly who held the family together. Valerie remembers her grandfather as a cold and distant old man whose meanness was a family joke and whose disinclination to hospitality and fun placed a damper on life at the Mote. There was also a religious element to Polly's upbringing which must have left its mark. Although Sir Thomas was a member of the Church of England, his father, Sir James Ranken Fergusson, was a strict Presbyterian who required his children, grandchildren and great grandchildren to make several church visits on Sundays when they visited him in Scotland. Known as 'Shoot-bang-gagger' because of his inclination to point his cane and imitate the sound of a gun when he disagreed with something, Sir James was not highly regarded by either Valerie or her brother Gilbert. Valerie remembers a visit to Scotland when she was about six as being a very dour business: 'We had to go to church three times on Sunday. We weren't allowed to play or read a book and we daren't speak at dinner. Even if you dared to speak there always seemed to be bagpipes playing in your ear.'

Ightham Mote is now owned by the National Trust. It is open to the public and is in the process of being extensively restored. When Valerie last visited the house in the summer of 1993, she found it difficult to imagine her mother being brought up there. The manor-house, which dates back to 1340, was built over a period of six hundred years. Its name is derived from the village of Ightham which is two miles north of the house. There is a moat around the building, but it is not clear if the 'Mote' is an earlier spelling of 'moat' or a version of the Anglo-Saxon word 'mot', meaning a meeting-place for the leading men of a locality.

Because it was built up through so many generations, Ightham Mote is almost an encyclopedia of six centuries of English architecture. It has seventy-two rooms, built mainly on two floors, all overlooking either the courtyard or the moat and gardens. The Mote has its own ghost, Dame Dorothy Selby, whose ancestors sold the house to Sir Thomas in 1889. Valerie remembers being terrified of Dame Dorothy when she used to stay at Ightham as a little girl. The Mote's colourful history was very real and quite scary to Valerie, who vividly recalls being told that during the English Civil War, a Roundhead soldier was pushed through a secret door into the moat and drowned because he'd come to ask for the hand of the daughter of the house: at that time the owner was a Cavalier. The Roundhead was not the only fatality at Ightham. When a doorway in the great hall, which had previously been blocked up, was opened in 1872, the seated skeleton of a young woman was found inside.

When it comes to the discussion of emotions and feelings, Valerie is minimalist; walking around Ightham Mote, in the course of research for her biography, it was obvious that the experience saddened her. 'It frightens me almost; it wasn't a cheerful style of living. Now it just gives me a feeling that I wouldn't want to live here.' But Polly did live there amidst a battery of servants and retainers in what was, by all accounts, a cheerless and lonely home, where she was not over-exposed to hospitable inclinations.

This was the background from which the young Polly Colyer-Fergusson approached her marriage to Walter Monckton. Hers was an inward-looking, unchanging and somewhat closed world, while his was the acquisitive, ambitious and socially gregarious domain of the new business class. Perhaps some of Walter's friends guessed that the pair were less suited than was superficially apparent, but for the citizens of Ightham and the surrounding countryside, Polly and Walter's wedding was an occasion for great celebration: 'When Walter and Polly left the church they were strewn with flowers by the inhabitants of Ightham. In the village was an air of rustic carnival. Flags and bunting from bygone flower shows and jubilees were out on the streets, and the couple drove through triumphal arches of rambler roses to the reception at Ightham Mote, where five hundred guests were awaiting them.'5

Walter and Polly had spent a couple of weeks of their honeymoon in the Chamonix valley in France when news of the declaration of war reached them. They returned to England immediately, though it was quite some time before Walter managed to get a commission. Despite approaches to the army, navy and the Royal Flying Corps, Walter had failed to gain entry into any of the services. He was regarded as unfit for war duty because of defective vision in one eye. Valerie is very proud of her father's efforts to ensure that he 'did his bit' and tells with pleasure the story of how Walter got into the 4th West Kent Regiment. Apparently the medical rules were less rigid in some units and luckily for Walter this was the case in the 4th West Kent, where both his brother Leslie and cousin Lance Monckton were officers. The two invited Walter for lunch in the mess and included the medical officer in the party. After a number of ports the acquiescent doctor told Walter to read the test cards with his good eye first, learn the letters off by heart, and then repeat the manoeuvre with his bad eye. Following this unusual charade, Walter was passed fit and given a commission. But he had not been idle in the months since returning from his aborted honeymoon. Walter had entered chambers in the Temple and had sat the General Examination of Students of Inns of Court in October 1914, thus putting his future legal career onto a sound footing before beginning his army life.

During the early part of the war, Walter was stationed in various locations in the south of England and was able to attend the christening of his son, born in November 1915. The child was named after Walter's best friend Gilbert Talbot and after Riversdale Colyer-Fergusson, Polly's brother. Sadly Gilbert, who was meant to have been the child's godfather, was killed at Hooge, while Riversdale was killed in action in 1917. For Walter, the war really began in June 1917 when he was finally posted to France. As his biographer points out, Walter was not a natural soldier: his eyesight and somewhat stressed disposition were not ideal attributes for a military man. Nevertheless his natural ability to win people's affection was a considerable bonus for him when he took up duty in October 1917, ' . . . in the appalling mud of the Salient at a difficult moment in the Third Battle of Ypres . . . . '

> During this time in the Salient, conditions were so horrible and so divorced from reality that frequently ordinary trenches could not be dug, and the troops existed miserably like animals in holes in the mud. It was in these circumstances that Walter showed his real calibre as an officer. He was conscientious to a fault in going out, whatever the conditions or danger, to visit and hearten the men shivering in these miserable pits and caked from head to foot in mud.[6]

This is just a glimpse of one man's experience of a war that was meant to indelibly define the horror of such conflict and therefore end all wars. Valerie was born two months before the Armistice, while her father was still in France, so the reader might well question the significance of describing Walter's war experience in a book about his daughter who grew up when the conflict was long over. But the war, and talk of it, was ever present in her childhood. Later, participation in World War II would dominate the first five years of her marriage.

What seems to have left an important mark on Valerie's psyche was the image of the slaughter and heroism of men on the battlefield. Now seventy-five years of age, she speaks with absolute recollection about her uncle Riversdale, who was posthumously awarded the Victoria Cross, and about her father's friends and their experience of the 'killing fields'. In her bungalow near the river Dargle in County Wicklow, there is a framed copy of her uncle Riv's VC, with his photograph and the inscription honouring his valour. Perhaps it is this combination of her admiration for the men who went to war and the intensity of her relationship with her father that has made Valerie a woman who appears more comfortable in the company of men.

When Valerie was born, on 12 September 1918, Polly was living in a little house just above Ightham village. Before Walter's embarkation for France she had moved several times in order to be near his post, but once he left she moved back to Ightham to be near both their families. Given the amount of time that Polly and Walter spent apart at this stage of their marriage, it is not surprising that no hint of strain appears in their correspondence. What is interesting about the letters Walter wrote to Polly and friends when he was in France was his preoccupation with religion. It is clear from a letter sent from the trenches, in the possession of Valerie's brother, Viscount Monckton, that Polly was reading a book about Catholicism in the summer of 1917: 'I'm not clear how far your book goes in saying that the unbaptised will never see God? I personally have never worried about that. I don't think that it is an essential tenet of Christianity really.' And later: 'Confession has many advantages, it is humiliating and makes you think of your faults. It is open to many abuses and that is why it was opposed by the Reformers. Bad clergy who gave way to what was confessed to are gone. Of course if you accept the Roman view they do further insist on the Sacrament of Penance. They say that repentance consists of three parts; confession, penance and new life. I have never made a practising confession. I'm always a little nervous of being too finicky and missing the big things.' Finally the letter concludes: 'There's a great attraction in living the whole Catholic life, nothing left to decide, but that may be cowardly. I should awfully like the *Catholic Faith* after you.'[7]

It wasn't just the terror and horrors of the battlefield that initiated Walter's interest in Roman Catholicism. Both Valerie and Gilbert agree that he had considered converting while still at Harrow. Again from France in July 1917 he wrote to his old Harrovian headmaster Lionel Ford:

> Your inspiration has got to come in the last resort from Jesus Christ, and all the difficulty I have about getting religion sufficiently *personal* is gradually going away out here. They don't seem to have washed our Romance from religion here. No long faces and black clothes but a jolly buoyant devotion in these little smashed churches, and smiling padres: and a wonderful wistful pathos in the Calvaries standing among the ruins. It has got all the humanity and sense of continuity of the Catholic Church.[8]

It would appear that Walter needed to be able to touch his God: perhaps he also needed the sense of individual personal drama more associated with the saving of the Catholic soul. Ironically, seventy-five years after this letter was written Valerie would say that she found it difficult to explain her own conversion to Roman Catholicism: 'somehow I felt closer to God in a Catholic church'. Gilbert's view is that his father 'was a bit too holy for such a young man who was only just married'. Though Walter never converted to Roman Catholicism, he followed the Anglo-Catholic rite for much of his life, while also preaching for a time at his own Church of England chapel at Ightham.

By all accounts Walter's later attraction to women did not feature while he was serving in France, and his cousin Lance Monckton wrote often from the Front about Walter's taking of the sacrament and general piety.[9] There can be no doubt that the tension between this strong religious impulse and the need for the company of women was there from the beginning. Gilbert highlights what was perhaps Walter's need to cleanse himself. 'You wouldn't believe what it meant to my father, being an Anglo-Catholic, he never slept with his wife during Lent and he went on retreats for a month to a place in Yorkshire.'

So what were the essential traits of the man who returned to his young wife and two children in the spring of 1919? As we have seen from his school reports he wanted to achieve: it is also evident that he wanted to be liked. He was a keen and able cricketer, but his outer joviality hid an inward-looking and contemplative disposition. An intense conflict raged within him; he thought much about his soul but frequently betrayed his own standards. Gilbert sees him as 'a lonely man. Work was like a drug for him. Ambition must have been the reason that he worked so hard'. In a sense it was this constant work and his inability to meet Polly in her world and on her terms that destroyed their marriage: but it was only half of the story.

When Walter came home from the war the family moved into a small house in Cleveland Place in London. Valerie's first memory is of her nanny, the unusually named Gwendolen Yelf, who would return to work for Valerie when she had her first child, Lingard. 'The only bad thing I can ever remember Nanny doing was pinching my cheeks. She'd always do that just before I went down to see my mother before tea. It would make me look healthier. You see, one didn't really see one's parents in those days. Now as I think of it, I can't imagine what the mothers did all day. But I didn't resent not seeing her. It was natural. That was the way it was. My nanny was number one then.

Honestly, my mother was number two because I was with Nanny all of the time. I remember the daily routine seemed to revolve around washing. It was all bustle. There was a cook, a parlour maid, Nanny and two nursery maids. I think we used to call them Big Bertha and Little Bertha. The nursery maid went to the kitchen for the food for Nanny and myself and Gilbert. And I remember that Nanny only washed my dresses and nice things but the nursery maid washed the nappies and later on the underwear.

'I was absolutely secure as a young child. Everything was ordered. After I was fed and washed in the morning, Nanny would put me into this great big pram and after she managed to get it down the steps of the house on Cleveland Place, she'd walk for miles. The routine was the same for all the nannies. They'd all meet up in Hyde Park. There was a great hierarchy about it all. The nannies who worked for a "Mr and Mrs" were not as important as the ones who worked for "Lord and Lady" this or that. I think that we came downstairs from the nursery at about four o'clock and we might stay until six. I can't remember much, but I think my father occasionally played with me, but I don't think there was much contact with my parents when I was little. I suppose I was let into their bed but I can't remember it. I think that all my affection was focused on Nanny. Looking back, the predominant feeling I have is that I was in awe of my mother. Papa was working so hard; one didn't laugh very much. It was very dull really. It wasn't a cheerful home. I suppose it didn't impinge though because I was so young.'

Valerie does not believe that naked ambition alone drove her father. But whatever the motivation, Walter was a man obsessed with work, almost to the exclusion of everything and everyone else. By the time it was decided that the family should move to the country he was already set in the pattern of behaviour that would dominate the rest of his life. In simple terms, Walter worked until he dropped: and when he dropped he would at last take the ease that both his mind and body needed. Polly must have hoped that the move to Kent in 1925 would bring with it a more normal home life. The move was possible because Walter had done exceedingly well at the Bar in his early years, though he was notorious for charging less than his colleagues. Once Polly had convinced him to listen to the advice of friends who recommended that he introduce a minimum fee, Walter's finances were at last secure and the couple bought land in Kent not far from Ightham, where they built a house which they called Fishponds. Valerie feels that her mother was longing to get her father out of London. There were fir trees surrounding the house at Fishponds and this, it was hoped, would be good for Gilbert's tuberculosis. While Fishponds was being built, the family moved in with Polly's father at Ightham Mote. Valerie remembers being 'beastly' to her step-grandmother, known as Aunt Mary. 'She had a maid called Posie whose only job was to look after her clothes. Posie and my nanny became great friends and went about together all the time. I don't think we children were really very nice to Aunt Mary.' It was interesting to note while walking around Ightham Mote with Valerie in 1993 that the pleasant or gentle memories of the place all related to Posie and Nanny.

Once Fishponds was ready there was much work for Polly, who set about reclaiming the garden which was overrun by heather and bracken. Walter meanwhile built stables and began riding with the West Kent Hunt every Saturday. This departure should have augured well for relations with Polly as she was also a good horsewoman, and at first they did hunt together. For Valerie this was a much happier time. 'There were more people around. Papa brought his "devils" down at weekends and there was much more social activity. There was Ightham cricket club and summer bathing at the ponds which were about a half mile from our house. Mother had a Baby Austin and we used to go around visiting people in it. I saw more of my mother then. I used to go to a little school run by the local rector's sister. There were just three other girls there. I don't think we learned much.' Valerie's memories of life in Kent revolve around her Arab pony, Sirdar, and the comings and goings of her frenetic father. She accompanied her father every morning to Kemsing station where he caught the 8.00am London train. Both Gilbert and Valerie recall that contact with their father was limited when he came home at about 7.00pm. He would eat his dinner and immediately retire to the study with his 'briefs' and a large box of biscuits.

Gilbert finds it easier than Valerie to discuss the breakdown of their parents' marriage. Of the two, Gilbert is more forthright about his father's infidelities, and more revealing about the effect it all had on Polly. 'My mother was a beautiful, caring person. She was a real mother. She didn't like the kind of chaps my father was going about with. His relaxation from tense work was the horse and the hunting field. He brought the hunting pals back to the house and often they were the worse for drink. My mother hated it all. She stopped riding altogether but he lived for it. Around then he went off with the master of the hunt's wife. That was the first woman.' Both Lord Birkenhead and H Montgomery Hyde, Monckton's biographers, have appeared to lean heavily on Polly in their analysis of the break-up:

> In her way she had been a good wife, looking after the house conscientiously, and bringing up the children well; but she showed him none of the personal warmth he needed; and the children apart, they had no shared interests of the kind which might have made mere companionship tolerable. They could not even enjoy a holiday together. Walter could no longer bear being at Polly's side with no work to distract him. In any case he had never liked travelling. Even in the early days of his marriage, he was inclined to cry off a family holiday at the last moment, pleading the pressure of work.[10]

Whatever about Polly's inhibitions, it seems cruel to place the burden of the failure of the marriage on her shoulders while ignoring the complexities of Walter's hyperactive and discordant personality. Valerie remembers that her father agreed to go on a cruise with Polly one summer, as long as the children went with them. 'He took stacks of briefs with him and sat on deck reading them all day. It must have infuriated her. She wanted fun and companionship but she got none. I think she was desperately fond of Gilbert so that helped, but it wasn't the same.' Valerie feels that her father's overwork was the biggest part of the problem. 'He didn't take her out much and when he did, he'd go off and dance with everyone else. She'd be desperately upset. She was shy and he rather left her aside. She didn't want the same kind of fun that he did. She needed to talk about children and the home. I suppose they weren't terribly in love; there was no passion there.' In simple terms, Walter was completely indifferent to the things that interested Polly; he took her home-making for granted and failed to see her loving creativity. For her part, Polly was incapable of responding to Walter's larger-than-life world, his intense professional activity and garrulous recreational carousing.

Valerie was about twelve before she realised that her mother and father were unhappy, but she was fourteen before she understood that the woman that her father was spending time with was more than a friend. 'I remember he would invite me to go places with them. I realised afterwards that I was there as a cover to make things look all right. Later I remember going to Holland with them and he told me that he was going to marry her. I was so unhappy that I told him that I would go home straight away. That stopped it; it was the worst thing that I ever did. She was a lovely person. If he'd married her, the first one, things would have been all right. Of course it would have been terrible for my mother no matter what. But things did get worse and worse.' Valerie says she cannot understand why her father, as she sees it, suddenly became interested in women. 'He was the last person that you'd expect to behave like that. He got all the peace and quiet that he needed at home.'

It would appear that because of her deep affection for her father, Valerie is blinded to the obvious. Gilbert, who was never at home as much as Valerie and was far more critical of Walter, took his mother's side. 'During the split in the family I was very much on my mother's side. In a sense I never knew my father. Walter got back after I had been sent to bed and left before I went to school. This affair with the hunting lady made my mother very low. So low that she tried to commit suicide. She took an overdose. As I remember I was about twenty at the time and in Cambridge. The family doctor rang me up and told me what had happened. The strange thing was that this doctor's father had delivered me in 1915 after he'd galloped over from Ightham to the Mote. Then twenty years later his son saved my mother. My father stayed away from me during that period. But he did try and explain it to me later. He took me to Brighton for the day once to tell me his side of the story. As we walked down the pier he said to me "Gilbert, I suffer from a terrible thing – I'm most attracted to women". Later, in about 1942, when he was in the Middle East handling propaganda for the Ministry of Information, my father had a relationship with a woman who the family used to call the "old grey mare". It was a most disgraceful time in his life. The ambassador had him in and told him it would have to stop.'

> While at the King David Hotel in Jerusalem he met Mrs Keith Newell, Commandant of the II Company of the Mechanical Transport Corps in the Middle East Forces. Mary Newell was an extremely good-looking woman, intelligent and self-assured. Women tended to dislike her, and those under her command felt that her only real interest lay in attracting attention to herself; but men fell for her,[11] and Walter was bewitched both by her beauty and by the way she seemed to 'add to the gaiety of life'. The inevitable affair followed.[12]
>
> His friendship with Mrs Newell, who had now openly moved into Beit el Azrak[13] where she arranged the social side of his life with great efficiency, had also become a matter of wide comment, and his extraordinary, if characteristic, indiscretion in also introducing her into his office caused an immediate protest by Arthur Rucker[14] when he returned from leave to find a staff seething with indignation.[15]

Valerie believes that Walter would have lived a more normal and settled life had she not objected to his wish to marry his hunting companion. One wonders if she is not indulging in just a little wishful thinking here. It appears that Walter Monckton was a man riven by conflicting emotional and intellectual forces: a man who thought and talked ceaselessly about God, spirituality and morality; but also a man who revelled in the company of the *bon viveur* and rakish women. Once permanently estranged from Polly, though not divorced, Walter had many relationships. In the early 1940s he had affairs with a number of well-known and beautiful actresses. One of them was Leonora Corbett, with whom he kept up an animated correspondence. He wrote to her about his daily routine, his work at the Ministry of Information where he had been appointed controller of censorship in October 1939, and even confided in her about his role in the 1936 abdication crisis, a subject he had refused to talk about, despite an offer of one hundred thousand pounds. But when Leonora went to America with Noël Coward's play, *Blithe Spirit*, it appears that Walter found another beau.

Leonora had a habit of addressing him as MDDDW, meaning My Darling, Darling, Darling Walter:

Hotel Pierre
New York
30 June 1941

D D Walter,

You haven't written to me for a long, *long* time – and I don't think you love
me anymore. In America ugly rumours of another woman have reached us –
and made me very sad, and bloody angry! Anyway I am happy you are back
'safe' in England – happier still if you will be a little 'unsafe' in America!

The Merry Wife of Windsor[16] – and her Royal husband honoured our play
with a visit – making me very happy by coming round in the 2nd interval. Our
talk was all of you – the Duke looked wonderful – sunburnt and blue – and
the Duchess was enchanting. They do so want you to come over. Would you?
This time their visit to the USA was well managed. Very little publicity and
all of it good. Our play runs on and on – a long tour following.

Please tell me about yourself Darling –

Lovingly always,
Leonora[17]

Leonora was right to be worried as Walter was indeed on friendly terms
with another actress, Alice Delysia. Alice was French, and during the
period of Walter's attachment to the Ministry of Information she was
playing in a revival of *The French For Love* by Marguerite Steen and
Derek Patmore. Later in early 1942 he would renew their affair while
she toured the Middle East entertaining the troops for ENSA.[18] On 25
February 1942 Walter noted in his Cairo diary: 'In Damascus we stayed
in the hotel and found Alice Delysia a charming and amusing
companion. We lunched with the President of the Syrian Republic,
Sheikh Taj Din, who was more curiously shaped than anyone I have
ever seen. He was like a gasometer placed on two others. Thank God I
procured some photographs in which we are together.'[19]

Valerie acknowledges her father's amours, though she obviously finds
their discussion exceedingly distasteful. Perhaps she overplays the
importance of her refusal to give her imprimatur when Walter
suggested that he would marry his first hunting companion, and wants
to believe that all would have been well had she not demurred. It is also
difficult for her to fully confront the reality of the pain that her mother

must have experienced during the break-up of the marriage, because in so doing she would have to acknowledge her father's cruelty. In that, she is no different from any child faced with the horrible dilemma of choosing between warring parents. Another factor that must have played its part in Valerie's perception of events was her mother's controlled behaviour. Valerie says that Polly 'was never physically fit. She was in bed for a couple of days every month' [because of her period]. It is also more than likely that she withdrew to her room as a means of avoiding the difficulties she faced in her marriage, in much the same way that Walter retired to his study every night, thereby avoiding contact with Polly. Valerie cannot remember any scenes, but does recall one incident that happened before she was sent to boarding school in the summer of 1933. 'I did go up to her room once and I found her in tears. She was just lying beside her bed crying. Then I realised that he'd told her that he was going to London for a few days but she must have realised that he was seeing *her*.'

Whatever about Valerie's perception of events, it must have been a period of intense stress for her parents. Walter had been appointed attorney general to the Prince of Wales in 1932 and the following year he became the constitutional adviser to the Nizam of Hyderabad, His Exalted Highness Sir Osman Ali Khan Bahadur Fatah Jung, GCSI, BBE. The Nizam was the leading Muslim ruler in India. His territory covered an area half the size of France and had a population of some sixteen million people. Walter had been recommended for the post by the retiring adviser, Sir Donald Somervell, whom he had known at Harrow. This was far from being a ceremonial office and would involve Walter in repeated visits to India during a most difficult period in the country's relations with Britain. As Walter's public and professional responsibilities mounted in 1933, he was growing further and further away from Polly as his relationship with his hunting friend intensified.

Gilbert had been at Harrow since he was seven, but Valerie had been educated locally or by a governess. No doubt the domestic difficulties at Fishponds played a part in the decision to send Valerie, who was by then fifteen, to a progressive and modern girls' school, Downe House, near Newbury. Her diary entry for Tuesday 19 September is somewhat terse: 'In the morning went to Sevenoaks. Then to Ightham. Then went to Cold Ash where Downe House is, it is eighty-five miles. It was rather nasty and overwhelming at first.' Valerie admits that she was no great scholar, though it was more than likely not her fault. Her early schooling had been somewhat irregular. After it was decided that she no longer required her much loved Nanny, a governess was appointed to take over her education. Valerie thinks that she probably got off to a bad start with the governess because of her sadness at losing Nanny. 'I think Papa understood how upset I was, more so than my mother. It was quite wrong for Nanny to go. It was like losing a best friend or a favourite aunt. I think it was then that father brought me a little dog called Trousers to cheer me up. But the governess didn't work out at all. She didn't like me and I didn't like her. I remember her saying "I can get you through any exam at any time if you learn things by rote". It was terrible. Even then I knew that I should understand things. Of course later I was always behind at proper school. After that I was sent to boarding school.'

Valerie did not like boarding school, as is clear from an inspection of her diary for the end of 1933. From her first day at Downe House she began noting how many days there were until the end of term. There were ninety-one days, beginning on 19 September. 'I didn't like being away from home at all. I was a bad pupil and had a very chequered career. Our classes were in forty-minute periods and when I had a "free forty", as we used to call it, I'd rush off to the library to read *Punch*. My best friend was Rosemary Garvey. She was way ahead of me and was very clever.' Rosemary now lives in a very remote part of Mayo, beyond Louisburgh, where she has retired to write and think and nurture a few animals. She remembers Valerie as a popular girl who was quite good at games but not too academic. 'She was never a bully. She was quiet and pretty and she didn't challenge people and was nice to all sorts of people. Her interests were riding, hunting and animals. Later on there were lots of young men who thought that Valerie was much fonder of them than she really was.' When Rosemary first knew Valerie her parents were still living together and she cannot recollect her talking about any difficulties at home. 'My impression of her father was, that although he was a Conservative, he was a socially-minded man. He was fair-minded and had a strong sense of fair play. By comparison with

Polly's background, Walter was much more democratic. I think that she was much more inhibited than Walter. But certainly the façade was kept up when Valerie was in school.'

As relations deteriorated at home, Walter often stayed at the Windham Club on St James's Square in London. He wrote to Valerie from his club on her first day at Downe House:

Var Darling,

Just to show I have not forgotten you yet. I am already looking forward to coming down to see you. I don't suppose you will be able to read a word of this, can you.[20]

I do hope you will like school, when you get used to it. Don't forget all the things we have learnt together. Our Lord always gave up everything for other people at his own expense – so don't always be thinking of yourself but be unselfish. I know you'll try. Don't forget all Father Philips said about Our Lady – 'Humility' that is, we must not take ourselves too seriously – we don't matter that much –'Purity' be careful about that. 'Obedience' that is, keep some discipline over yourself and stick to the best that is in you.

What a pie-jaw! But it is best to think straight about the things that matter from the start.

You will enjoy yourself. I shall think of you every day, night and morning and at other times, because I love you so. Write sometimes, you little spud.

T. W. E. A. T: S. Y. L: Live and let live. I doubt it said the carpenter. Way horse, way.

Always your very loving Daddy.[21]

According to Valerie, the somewhat incomprehensible second last line of the letter was part of a private language that she shared with her father. Apart from the obvious warmth and affection in the letter, it highlights once again the conflict between Walter's expressed piety and his personal behaviour. Though not now regarded by either herself or her friends as a great letter-writer, Valerie seems to have kept up a good correspondence with her father while she was at school.

It was around this time that Polly began to visit Italy. She loved Tuscany and was lucky enough to make friends with an American man on one of her visits. Valerie feels that the gentleman may have been homosexual and this provided Polly with friendship and companionship without the problem of gossip. In a letter from Walter concerning how she should spend the Easter holidays, there's just a hint of the loneliness Valerie must have felt, with her father in London and her mother in Italy. Dated 1 March 1934, the letter was sent from the Windham Club:

> Var Darling,
>
> Thank you for your letter. Of course I want you for Easter, you little beast. So arrange it. Have I to write to Miss Willis?
>
> I had a telegram this morning from Mummy to say they had arrived safely.[22]

The word 'activism' is often used when people describe Valerie's qualities. Her friend Rosemary Garvey says it is the key to an understanding of her life, while Dr A J F O'Reilly sees her as a 'benign activist'. That quality is there in the images from her childhood. Photographs show her 'doing something': she is always on a horse, wicket keeping, or holding jumble sales for the local charity. An undated cutting from a Sevenoaks newspaper reads: 'Gilbert and Valerie Monckton have not long been members of the League, but they have already shown that they are keenly interested in our work. On April 20th they held a Jumble Sale and sent us £8.10s.11d. as the result. Through their instrumentality also several new Members have been enrolled.'[23] Her diary for 1933 shows a young woman who was either out riding, walking, playing netball, 'practising lacrosse', recording her school cricket teams batting averages or else going to or from chapel:

> In the morning went to chapel. Then went and had to write out timetables. Had French lesson. Pretty disgusting. Had a spare 40. Then English prep. Latin lesson. Jolly nice. Had lunch then next. Then learned to play lacrosse. Then had one more 40. Tea. 3 more 40s. Chapel. Supper. Then played cards with Olive Wilson and Margaret Swan.[24]

The somewhat staccato, matter-of-fact tone of Valerie's juvenile diary reflects accurately the style of the adult woman. Things are either 'jolly good' or 'pretty disgusting': life is black and white, but whatever it is, one gets on with it. As Rosemary Garvey recalls, Valerie's 'can do' qualities were there from the very beginning. 'She never analysed things. She simply got on and did things.'

If Dr O'Reilly is correct in attributing Thatcher-like qualities to Valerie, then there can be no doubt that the single-mindedness, ambition and determination were all inherited from her father. When Dr O'Reilly describes her as part Florence Nightingale and part sergeant-major, he is placing her in the sociocultural context of the class into which she was born: a class that 'was educated to go out and run the Empire. Valerie is part of that class. In another marriage she might have been the Vicereine of India'.

1 J C Moss, house master at Harrow to Walter's father, 1 August 1910. Monckton Papers, Bodleian Library Oxford. Dep. Monckton Trustees 1, F, 118–20.
2 *Walter Monckton*. H Montgomery Hyde, p5.
3 Dep. Monckton Trustees 1, F, 118–20.
4 *Walter Monckton: The Life of Viscount Monckton of Brenchley*. Lord Birkenhead, pp8, 9.
5 *Ibid*. pp41, 42.
6 *Ibid*. pp49, 50.
7 Shown to the author by the 2nd Viscount Monckton of Brenchley.
8 *Walter Monckton: The Life of Viscount Monckton of Brenchley*. Lord Birkenhead, p47.
9 *Ibid*.
10 *Walter Monckton*. H Montgomery Hyde, p36.
11 A letter in a private collection from 'Barbara', who served under Mary Newell, to Sir William Charles Crocker MC, 30 May 1969 and quoted in *Walter Monckton*. H Montgomery Hyde, p119.
12 *Ibid*.
13 Walter's villa in Cairo, lent by Chester Beatty.
14 The *chef de cabinet* in Cairo.
15 *Walter Monckton: The Life of Viscount Monckton of Brenchley*. Lord Birkenhead, p201.
16 A reference to the Duke and Duchess of Windsor, the former Edward VIII and Mrs Simpson.
17 Dep. Monckton Trustees 9, F, 14–16–55.
18 Entertainment National Services Association.
19 Dep. Monckton Trustees 9, F, 14–16–55.
20 Walter was referring to the fact that his writing was notoriously illegible.
21 A letter in Lady Goulding's possession.
22 *Ibid*.
23 An undated cutting from a Sevenoaks newspaper in Lady Goulding's possession.
24 Lady Goulding's diary for Thursday 21 September 1933.

2

A WINDOW ON THE EYE
OF THE STORM

No one will ever really understand the story of the King's life [Edward VIII]
during the [abdication] crisis who does not appreciate two factors: The first,
which is superficially acknowledged by many of those who were closely
concerned in the events of these days, was the intensity and depth of the
King's devotion to Mrs Simpson. To him she was the perfect woman. She
insisted that he should be at his best and do his best at all times, and he
regarded her as his inspiration. It is a great mistake to assume that he was
merely in love with her in the ordinary physical sense of the term. There was
an intellectual companionship, and there is no doubt that his lonely nature
found in her a spiritual comradeship.[1]

Walter Monckton's sensitive account of the relationship
between King Edward VIII and the twice-married Mrs Wallis
Simpson reflects both the friendship and trust that he shared
with the king as well as his own particular awareness of the need for
'spiritual comradeship'. Walter was in a position to pen an account of
the whole affair because he played a central role, advising Edward and
liaising between the king and the government during the autumn and
winter of 1936. Because of the delicacy of the matter, Walter asked
Valerie to act as a courier between Downing Street and Fort Belvedere,
the Berkshire folly to which Edward had retreated as he grew more
uncomfortable with life at Buckingham Palace. In turning her into a
messenger, Walter gave Valerie a window on the eye of the storm.
Barely eighteen, she not only met the king and Mrs Simpson, but she
observed them as they grappled to resolve the crisis which had resulted
from the king's insistence that he 'found it impossible to carry the

heavy burden of responsibility and to discharge my duty as King as I would wish to do, without the help and support of the woman I love'.[2]

Over the years many newspaper articles have been written about Valerie's role in the abdication crisis: most have created the impression that she somehow played a central role and that she was privy to secrets that she had been sworn to keep. In reality the true story is far more interesting than the public relations fairytale. King Edward would have been mad to have discussed the intimate details of the crisis with an eighteen-year-old girl and, of course, he didn't: Valerie never claimed that he did. Her claim to fame is that she had the great luck to be a fly on the wall during one of the most dramatic moments in the history of Britain's royal family. From her father's perspective she was the ideal choice; just like the three wise monkeys she saw no evil, heard no evil and could be relied upon to speak no evil. If Valerie does have secrets in her chest of memories, they are the opinions and impressions of her father rather than any set of confidential top-secret memos.

That said, she is the only person alive who witnessed Winston Churchill's emotional support for his king at Fort Belvedere; and she alone lurked in the shadows in the drawingroom at the Fort as prime minister Stanley Baldwin, with tears in his eyes, begged Edward not to abdicate. Valerie's memories provide a fascinating glimpse of the glamour and the drama of the events surrounding the abdication, but the reader should also note the effect it must have had on the maturation of this young woman. Chatting with her king, running in and out of Downing Street and taking advice about her future career from Churchill must have more than prepared Valerie for her role as the 'beggar-woman of Wicklow', as Dr O'Reilly likes to describe her fund-raising activities. Valerie has always been at home with the mighty of the earth and she is never intimidated: as a result there is absolutely no-one that she wouldn't approach and ask for funds for the Central Remedial Clinic.

Walter Monckton first met the Prince of Wales when both men were undergraduates at Oxford. David, as he was then called, attended a debate at the Oxford Union in February 1913 and sat beside Walter, who was president of the famous debating society. Walter had made one of his best speeches in late 1912 when he had opposed the Home Rule proposals in the presence of the Irish Parliamentary Party's William Redmond. However, on the day that the Prince of Wales attended, Walter had to do his best to present the Union in a lively and interesting light. Walter's relationship with the prince moved onto a professional footing when he was appointed as his attorney general in 1932; after David's accession to the throne, the office extended to the Duchy of Cornwall. Valerie remembers that she first met the prince at the end of 1935. 'I went down to the Duchy in Dartmoor with my father, where we helped the prince and his men round up the ponies. He would come down from London for the day and it was obvious that he enjoyed it. He was definitely happy on the moor. We'd go off to a pub at lunchtime and have some lunch. He spoke to my father mainly but he also spoke to me; it was all very ordinary. The talk was about land and farms. It was all very relaxed. I mean, there were detectives there, but we were all out in the air. He was very interested in people then; he hadn't gone overboard about Mrs Simpson at that stage.' Valerie doesn't remember feeling any sense of awe. 'It didn't seem odd to be speaking to the future king of England.'

Valerie was and still is very pro-king. She reveres Edward VIII's memory and refuses to read anything that might damage his reputation. Her preference for royal males has not diminished: Valerie breaks into loud mutterings when Princess Diana's name is mentioned. 'My father used to talk to me about the prince long before the abdication crisis. He always said that the generals had tried to prevent him from going to the front lines during the First World War. My father said that he was very different to his brothers: he had great feeling for the people. When he went to Wales and met the miners in 1936 the politicians were angry. He told the unemployed men in the collieries that something had to be done for them. That annoyed the government.'

A number of factors combined to propel Valerie into the unusual position of unofficial messenger to the king. In normal circumstances the new monarch would have leaned more heavily on the advice of his private secretary and the court advisers; unfortunately David, who took the name Edward on his accession to the throne, did not develop good relations with the courtiers and advisers he had inherited from his father, George V. The rumblings in court circles about Edward's behaviour began very shortly after the death of George V on 20 January 1936. The relationship between the prince and Mrs Simpson was not the only matter of concern: the old guard at the palace frowned upon the new king's social milieu, his more relaxed style and his perceived political views. Convinced that communism posed the greatest threat to Europe's future, Edward appeared to ignore the authoritarianism of National Socialism in Germany, and publicly admired its economic achievements. It was an open secret that successive German ambassadors to London had been instructed to cultivate him. Matters came to a head during the abdication crisis when Major Alexander Hardinge, the principal private secretary at the time, decided to write to Edward warning him, in terms that to Hardinge seemed measured and sympathetic and to the king brutally offensive, 'that the government were growing alarmed at his relationship with Mrs Simpson, that an approach would shortly be made to him which – if rejected – might lead to the government's resignation, and that the silence of the press could not last much longer and would probably break within the next few days'. Hardinge ended with a plea that Mrs Simpson should leave the country without any delay.[3]

Following this letter, relations between the king and his private secretary deteriorated even further. From then on, Edward completely excluded Hardinge and asked Walter Monckton to be his confidant and adviser. Fortunately for Edward, Walter was on good terms with both Hardinge and his aide, Sir Godfrey Thomas. Walter wrote in his memoir:

> My long friendship with Hardinge and Thomas made the inherent difficulties of our position easier where loyalties were hard to reconcile and petty acerbities not always easy to repress; above all, I think we trusted and understood each other where there were inevitable reticences. I used to think that Hardinge took too pessimistic and critical a view of the King's conduct; I am sure that he expressed his opinion too emphatically and widely to have any hope of retaining the King's confidence when the crisis came. The result was that the King was confirmed in his policy of not confiding his feelings and ideas on this subject to any of his staff.[4]

A copied fragment of a letter from Edward to Walter, in the possession of the Goulding family, provides a remarkable insight into the closeness of the relationship between the king and his adviser and friend:

> I really do apologise for giving you so much trouble when I know how hard you are driven in your job. But I should hate to have to put myself in anyone else's hands, not only because you have proved yourself a true friend but because no-one else knows me so well or what I'm up against. But you won't hesitate to tell me if it's inconvenient or for some reason the least bit tricky to have me stop in your house as I could easily go to a hotel.

When the crisis reached its apogee in October-November 1936, Walter almost single-handedly represented the king in his relations with both the Baldwin government and the rest of the royal family. But he needed help: he needed someone who could pass unnoticed in and out of Fort Belvedere, Downing Street and Buckingham Palace itself, if necessary. Valerie was only too delighted to help her father and more than willing to abandon her other activities.

Valerie has always maintained, though the dates do not altogether support her contention, that her father allowed her to leave Downe House so that she could come to London and assist him in his affairs with the king. 'I know I wrote to him and told him that I was miserable and that I wanted out. It was terrible: I never saw my brother and by then [late 1935] the family were back in London in a small flat on William Street near Knightsbridge. I remember he indicated vaguely that there was something coming up and that I would be able to help him. I just thought "thank God he's going to get me out of here". I think that it was then that I went off and learned shorthand and typing at the Monkey Club.' Though Walter's role was crucial in the eventual resolution of the king's dilemma, it seems unlikely, though possible, that Walter anticipated some sort of difficulty or crisis before the death of George V in January. If Valerie's recollection of events is correct, then as early as December 1935, as George V was dying, Walter must have expected that Edward would call upon his services. At any rate Valerie put Downe House behind her at the end of the Christmas term in 1935, though it was the following October before she had the honour of serving both her father and her king.

However, there is no doubt that Walter's intimacy predated the crisis itself. In his memoir he noted a series of meetings between himself and Edward when George was ill, as well as in the first weeks of the new king's reign:

> He spoke very frankly to me, as a friend, of his worries. He could not bear to feel that he would be cooped up in Buckingham Palace all the time within the iron bars. They must take him as he was – a man different from his father and determined to be himself. He would be available for public business and public occasions when he was wanted, but his private life was to be his own and was, as far as possible, to be lived in the same way as when he was Prince of Wales. The Fort[5] was to remain a retreat for weekends and for rest. He never spoke to me of any doubt or hesitation about accepting his position as King. It was only later on in the year, when the controversy was upon him, that he would sometimes say that if they were wanting someone exactly reproducing his father, there was the Duke of York [his brother].[6]

The sympathy Walter Monckton felt for Edward VIII must surely have emanated from some sense of identification with a man who shared to some degree his difficulties with women. The Prince of Wales had been involved in many love affairs long before he met Mrs Simpson. Many of the women he saw were married. In fact it was Lady Thelma Furness, whom Mrs Simpson once described as the 'Princess of Wales', who introduced Wallis to the future king. Lady Furness wrote in her memoirs that while on safari in 1930 'the Prince's tent was always on one end of the line and mine next to his, and we shared a fire'.[7] It must have been very convenient for Thelma Furness, but perhaps not quite so comfortable for her husband, who was also on safari.

Although he was 'seeing' Lady Furness, the prince was still writing to Freda Dudley Ward, from various African locations. He had first met Mrs Dudley in 1918, and from 1919 on appears to have had a genuine, warm friendship and passionate love affair with her. Freda was a good woman, married to a man sixteen years her senior, who tolerated the relationship as long as it was conducted with decorum and discretion. Looking back, and talking about it as if it were yesterday, Valerie says that the prince would have been 'all right' if he had remained involved with Freda Dudley Ward. She had a young family of girls whom 'David visited throughout most of the twenties'. It was a private-public relationship where her influence was generally regarded as good. For

Valerie, the most important thing was that Freda never spoke publicly about the relationship, even after her lover of nearly fifteen years refused to take her calls when the relationship with Mrs Simpson began. 'That must have been awful for her. Can you imagine? She was used to ringing Buckingham Palace whenever she liked. The staff knew to put her through immediately. Then without any notice the palace told her that they'd been instructed not to take her calls. How awful!' Valerie expresses a view of Mrs Dudley Ward that appears in several biographies. 'Freda was a good influence. She was interested in the poor and in people's problems. And she encouraged him to be concerned about it. I think that was one of the reasons why he was so fond of her.'

Unlike many of David's contemporaries and many historians, Valerie is convinced that David did want to be monarch. 'He had done his time. I think he honestly did want to be king. He felt he could do something for the poor. He wanted Parliament to act. I don't know if he knew what should be done but he did want something done. Freda Dudley Ward encouraged him to think he could do something. Later, some of his other friends weren't interested in that sort of thing. They just wanted fun. I do believe that he could have been a successful king. It was probably better that the Yorks took over in the end, but he could have made a terrific success of the throne if he'd been able to dampen down his ardour about certain types of woman. It was his flaw. If he'd stuck quietly to Freda Dudley Ward, nobody would have said anything. He should have stuck to her and remained a proper king. She never wrote her story or went about talking about their love affair. It was her brother who talked to me about how sad she was.'

Valerie says that when her father first spoke to her about the job that he had in mind for her, she had not heard the rumours concerning the king's relationship with Mrs Simpson. 'I think it was in his chambers that he said to me – "There's something coming up and I know that you can keep quiet. Whatever I tell you, you must keep it to yourself". It was probably early October 1936. He had just come back from Hyderabad because the king had sent him a telegram asking for his help.' It seems odd that Valerie can't remember having heard the gossip, because Mrs Simpson was at the palace when, as a young debutante, Valerie was presented in the spring of 1936. But given her age and her undoubted innocence it is possible that it passed over her head. It had not, however, passed over the heads of those in the upper echelons of the government and court circles. Long before 1936 Walter had been approached by Lord Wigram, George V's private secretary, who told him of his concern about the future king's relationship with Mrs Simpson. In February 1936 Walter was once again approached by senior government figures who told him that Ernest Simpson, Wallis's husband, had let it be known that the king had made him aware of his feelings for his wife as well as his desire to marry her. By the spring, Edward had thrown all caution to the wind: court circles were not amused to read the Simpsons' names in the *London Gazette*, which reported their presence at a dinner party given by the king. In April, Walter heard rumours of Mrs Simpson's divorce proceedings and by the summer he was organising legal representation for Wallis.

By this stage London's inner circle were agog with the gossip, though the issue was still under wraps and had not been alluded to in the newspapers. Walter was seriously concerned about the consequences for the king should the relationship become a major issue. He wrote in his memoir:

> I didn't know to whom to turn. Eventually I decided to ask Mr Winston Churchill, whom the King liked and I knew slightly, for advice. He was not in the Government or Court circles so that it was easier to go to him. He was extraordinarily sympathetic and ready to help. Up and down his room in Morpeth Mansions he walked and talked. I can hear him now: 'Life is a tease. Joy is the shadow of sorrow, sorrow the shadow of joy'. He told me how he refused to sit at table with people who criticised the King. But he was plainly anxious about what I told him. He was all against divorce proceedings in which he saw no advantage; the presence of Mr Simpson was a safe-guard. Moreover he was anxious that I should make plain to the King how important it was that his friendship should not be flaunted in the eyes of the public. He particularly said that Mrs Simpson should not go as a guest to Balmoral.[8]

Edward's response to this advice and concern was to take Mrs Simpson on a cruise around the Mediterranean with an entourage that did not include her husband. The American newspapers had a field day with the king's indiscretion, and once again Walter stepped into the fray to prevent the British press doing likewise. He was lucky to have the assistance of Lord Beaverbrook, the press baron, who had decided to uphold the king's right to see whoever he liked. Afterwards Randolph Churchill asked Beaverbrook why he had taken the king's side and so vehemently opposed Stanley Baldwin's government during the crisis: 'To bugger Baldwin' was the alleged terse response.

Walter had come back from Hyderabad at the king's request. At that time, Mrs Simpson began to become seriously concerned by the newspaper coverage in the United States. But with her divorce proceedings due for hearing in late October, the whole matter reached the point of no return when Stanley Baldwin arrived back from holidays to his Downing Street desk to find a file of American press reports speculating on the likelihood of Wallis becoming queen of England. Mr Baldwin decided that he had to do something, and therefore sought a meeting with the king. It was at this point that Valerie was called upon and her walk-on part in the drama began. 'I thought that Mrs Simpson was going to be terrible. The impression I had of her, without having met her, was that she would be unpleasant. When I met her I was surprised by her definite attempt to be nice to me. If you think about it from her point of view, I mean, here was this young girl, just eighteen, now she didn't want me talking about her business. But she knew my father was fond of me and trusted me and that the king trusted my father. I imagine she said to herself "I'll do my best to get on with this brat". Not that she put it that way. But she never spoke down to me.' Despite the fact that many newspaper articles have inflated her role in the affair, often creating the image of a girl who actually played an active part in advising the king, Valerie says that she had no sense of doing anything important. 'My contact with the whole business was through my father. I was not involved in the discussions. My job was simply to be available to help my father and to carry messages. I can't remember now whether my mother even knew then that I was going up and down to the Fort.'

Once Stanley Baldwin met the king on 20 October, his fate could no longer remain undecided. From then on, the matter was being dealt with on an official, albeit discreetly official, basis, but the snowball was gathering momentum. Looking back, Valerie realises that there was never any real hope that a man like Baldwin would be able to make Edward VIII understand his perspective. 'He was so Victorian. He could never have understood that he [the king] would actually give up the throne.' Though very amicable at the time, the first meeting between the prime minister and the king proved disastrous because both men came away believing that their point of view had been understood. Nothing could have been further from the truth. Once Mrs Simpson was granted her decree nisi, Edward moved swiftly to make his position absolutely clear to Walter Monckton:

> The King told me one evening, sitting in the Empire Room at Buckingham Palace which he used as his sitting-room, that he intended to marry Mrs Simpson when she was free. Although I had not taken the view that his mind was made up in this direction, I cannot say that the news came as a shock to me. When the King told me of his decision I suggested that he might wait before taking any steps to act on a determination which could not in any event be given effect until the end of April 1937 (when the decree nisi would be absolute). But I could see at once that he did not agree with this advice because he felt that he could not go forward to the Coronation on 12 May 1937 meaning in his heart to make the marriage whatever happened and, as he felt, deceiving the Government and the people into imagining that he had dropped the association or, at any rate, did not intend to marry.[9]

The second meeting between Baldwin and the king took place on 16 November at Buckingham Palace, during which the prime minister told Edward that the proposed marriage would not be approved of by either Great Britain or the Dominions. In reply, the king told Baldwin that he was prepared to go in order to marry Mrs Simpson. Later that week, Walter was approached in the House of Lords by a barrister who was close to Baldwin, and asked if he would be prepared to act as channel of communication between the prime minister and the king. Once Walter was, in effect, representing the view of both parties, Valerie's usefulness was at a premium.

'The first really important letter I carried was from the king, who was at the Fort, to Number 10. I believe it was a royal summons. I used to drive to and from London in my old open-topped pink Morris Minor. It was called George. Well, as I was driving by the palace I was stopped by the police for speeding. They asked me where I was going but I couldn't tell them because it was all so 'hush-hush'. So I was fined. It was funny really but I said nothing and just continued on my way. I remember I took Baldwin's reply back to the Fort, where I sat in the drawingroom awaiting instructions. Baldwin arrived very quickly to see the king. He stood there with these big lugubrious eyes. I remember he wouldn't sit down. He was almost crying as he talked with my father and Edward. I can't remember his exact words but he was saying something like "don't do this to your country". Essentially he was begging the king to try and find some way of stopping it all. I just tried to drift out of the room without making any noise.' Valerie now finds it hard to remember the precise days on which the various meetings that she witnessed took place. But she remembers vividly the emotion of it all and the great sense of sadness. 'I was there and do remember the king telling Baldwin that he would abdicate. I knew that this was a possibility already because my father had told me. Baldwin was definitely crying and saying don't. The king just said "I have made up my mind". It was terribly sad.'

The next turn of the screw was the suggestion that the king and Mrs Simpson would agree to a morganatic marriage. In such a marriage the commoner remains 'common' and the children of such a union have no rights of succession or inheritance. Walter thought that the morganatic solution was not feasible and advised Edward of his view. Once again Baldwin met the king, and on being pressed about the proposal, told him that he thought that neither the Dominions nor Parliament would agree to the proposal or the legislation that would have to be enacted. From that point on, the issue became highly political and the king's fate was sealed. Having asked Baldwin to request the opinion of the Dominions' prime ministers about the choice he faced, Edward had effectively boxed himself in and was now reliant on their response. Rejecting Mrs Simpson as queen or a morganatic marriage, the Dominions favoured abdication.

During the crisis, and especially in relation to the morganatic proposal, Valerie's impression of Mrs Simpson was that she simply didn't understand the rules. 'She was American. She didn't understand England or the English. The morganatic thing was not a solution. I don't think she read history. Henry VIII and his marital arrangements was the depth of her knowledge of English history. She didn't understand the situation she was in. I don't know if she fully appreciated that he really did intend to marry her, because when she went to France, that was it. He wasn't going to let her go. I don't think she realised that her going was the end for him. They had to be separate for six months in order that her divorce would go through unchallenged. I believe that she truly thought that once the divorce was through that she could just come back. I think that in the end it all boiled down to the fact that she was twice fallen. I mean one divorce was plenty but can you imagine the queen of England with two previous marriages?'

At the end of November, Mrs Simpson was forced to abandon the London home that the king had acquired for her, because of abusive mail and some stone-throwing. Then, following a speech delivered by the bishop of Bradford, in which Edward's religious commitment was questioned, it became clear that the British press could no longer remain muzzled. Mrs Simpson, who was at that stage staying at Fort Belvedere, became very agitated and decided to flee to France. Valerie has vivid memories of Wallis's last day at the Fort. In June 1993 the Canadian millionaire Galen Weston and his Irish wife, Hilary, who now own Fort Belvedere, invited Valerie to visit the house and its grounds. Walking into the diningroom Valerie was immediately able to place the king, Mrs Simpson, her father and herself in the positions they had occupied at their last lunch together. 'I remember it so well. She was going to leave that afternoon for Cannes. Everyone was talking about nothing to avoid talking about what was on everyone's mind. I think she was very gracious. I mean she called the king "Sir" in my presence, which was the right thing to do. And she did talk to me. I wasn't left out. One really nice thing happened: when I came into the diningroom there were four bottles of beer sitting next to my place. The king had had them placed there. He had remembered that when we were rounding up the ponies on Dartmoor, the previous year, that I had had a beer in the pub and he had then remarked that I was very young to be drinking. It was very touching that he remembered on such a day . . . Then after lunch Mrs Simpson said that she wanted to talk to the king and my father alone, so I went off to the drawingroom and sat alone and waited. I was dying to go to the loo but I just sat there, I was too afraid to ask. Later I said goodbye to her and I left for London with my father. I don't know what he was thinking as we drove up but he must have felt awful.'

Valerie believes that the abdication could still have been prevented had Mrs Simpson meant what she said when she spoke to Edward from France, where she was being pursued by the press. 'She rang very often and the calls were very long. Often the line was bad. First she told him that she hadn't realised all that would happen and told him not to abdicate. Had she really meant it I think it is possible that the abdication process could have been stopped. I often wonder about her. I do believe that she thought she could be queen, but after she left for France she must have begun to realise that she couldn't be. I think that Edward on the other hand realised that Wallis could not be queen quite early on. But once he made up his mind to marry her he knew that his brother George would be king.'

Wallis Simpson left for France on 2 December, and the following day Walter replaced her as the king's companion at the Fort. Walter noted in his memoir that he felt Edward was under great strain and should be left alone. Over the next few days, Edward became convinced that he should broadcast to the nation and then go away for a time while the country digested what he had said. He also sought and was granted permission to meet Winston Churchill, who subsequently dined twice at the Fort on Friday and Saturday. Churchill advised delaying tactics and proffered the view that it was possible that Edward might win the battle with the government. Meanwhile the Cabinet, or sections of it, was in almost constant discussion of the issue as the crisis neared its end. Various proposals, including Walter's suggestion of two Bills, one allowing the king to renounce the throne and another making the Simpson decree nisi absolute immediately, were rejected. On 8 December Mrs Simpson issued a statement from Cannes in which she appeared to give up the king for the good of England, and on the same day Baldwin asked Walter to accompany him to the king's retreat where they should once again try to make Edward come to his senses.

Once again when the audience took place I was present with the Prime Minister and the King. The Prime Minister was a little deaf when he was tired, and on this occasion it had a curious result, as when the Prime Minister had urged once again all that he could to dissuade the King, for the sake of the country and all that the King stood for, from his decision to marry, the King wearily said that his mind was made up and he asked to be spared any more advice on the subject. To my astonishment, Mr Baldwin returned to the charge with renewed vigour and, I thought, put the position even better than before. He asked me immediately afterwards if I thought he had said all he could, and when I explained that I thought he had done even more, it was plain that he had not heard the King's request to him to desist.

The audience took place in the drawing-room with its large windows facing the garden and looking away to the woods. I can see them sitting there now, the King in his chair in front of the fire, Mr Baldwin at right angles to him on the sofa, and myself on a chair between them. It was the room in which the Abdication was to be signed in three days' time.[10]

Walter was by this stage simply trying to get the best terms possible for Edward: attempting to ensure his rank and financial security. On the night of 9 December Walter carried the king's formal decision back to Downing Street and set about drafting the message to parliament. Later that night he went to Marlborough House to see Edward's brother, the future George VI, and his mother, Queen Mary. In the early hours he arrived at Fort Belvedere, where the king had already been told of the Cabinet's decision that he must leave England for at least two years. Later that morning, the Dukes of York, Gloucester and Kent arrived to witness the copies of the abdication document and the address to Parliament. In the company of Sir Edward Peacock, who was the receiver general of the Duchy of Cornwall, Walter carried the papers to Buckingham Palace where their contents were to be cabled to the various Dominions. On Friday morning Winston Churchill travelled to the Fort, where he added some embellishments to Walter's draft of the king's broadcast message. Valerie often quotes Churchill's now infamous reciting of the lines from the poet Marvell on Charles I, as Winston said goodbye to the king:

He nothing common did or mean
Upon that memorable scene.

When the moment came to explain to the people why he had to go,

Edward found himself once again in the company of Walter Monckton. The broadcast was made from Windsor Castle:

> At 10 o'clock Sir John Reith came in and stood over the King, who sat before the microphone, and announced 'His Royal Highness Prince Edward' and left the room. The King began, I thought, a little anxiously, but with the sentences his confidence grew, and the strength of his voice, and the final sentence 'God Save The King' was almost a shout. When it was over the King stood up and, putting his arm on my shoulder, said: 'Walter, it is a far better thing I go to'.[11]

Valerie had agreed to go to the Haymarket theatre that Friday night with a young man called David Buzzard. On the day before his broadcast, she saw the king for the last time until after the war. She remembers telling her companion that they would have to miss the middle act as she wanted to go to the Carlton Club to listen to the radio at about ten o'clock. Needless to say Mr Buzzard thought it a waste of the tickets. 'Then the penny dropped. I more or less knew what he was going to do and say but I didn't really feel like going back to the theatre after it was over.'

Looking back, Valerie still sees Edward VIII as the victim: 'I thought the king was marvellous and so thoughtful, except where women were concerned. He was very good to my father though he used him night and day. But she was hard. She wasn't my type at all. She was so unable to understand the difference between America and England. You know there could have been fighting, a king's camp. But he wasn't going to let that happen. He abdicated to avoid that. But he was wrong to have put her before the throne. He should have put the country first. Yes, Edward was the naughty one. She must have had something that his other women didn't have. It must have come down to sex. She was terribly *soignée* and exciting. I think, with her American phraseology and ways, she was very exotic to him. When it came down to it, it was sex appeal. I couldn't understand the attraction.' Valerie feels that her father would have regarded Wallis sympathetically but 'he would have thought that she behaved without strength of character. She wasn't giving up the throne – she was giving up a man who would be king. Yet she could still see him. That wouldn't have been terrible. I remember when we had the debutantes' garden party and we were presented to the king, she was there standing right behind him. That annoyed people. I think it was palpable on the day.

'The royal household were not very nice about her. Edward's mother, Queen Mary, was very upright. She just looked down her nose at her. She was right not to receive her. You weren't even allowed into the royal enclosure at Ascot in those days if you were divorced. I think one divorce was quite enough for Queen Mary, but two! My father was very fond of her. He wrote to her immediately when he got back from Portsmouth having said goodbye to the king. She wrote back straight away and they met that day. She appreciated what my father had done. George VI made Papa a knight immediately after his accession. Father was delighted. He thought that some people felt that he had acted wrongly. But somebody had to act for the king and friendship was his primary motive. Many people were very critical. I think he was hurt by that. But all sorts of people abandoned the Duke and Duchess of Windsor (as they became) and the people who had been in their circle. But George VI didn't cut people off. He was grateful to my father for what he had done.'

Walter's association with Edward was far from over. As relations deteriorated between the duke and duchess and King George and the rest of the royal family, Walter was called upon again and again to act as an intermediary. It was an unhappy period for the duke who felt that his family had reneged on both the spirit and the financial terms of the agreement that had been drawn up on his behalf by Walter and the government. Valerie says that her father found his position difficult, especially during the period just before the war when both George VI and the government perceived the duke and duchess as a diplomatic liability. 'My father felt that he had fallen down on something that he wanted to do for David, and he couldn't understand why King George, who was such a nice man, could not just have said that Wallis had the same status as her husband. She was a duchess because she was married to a duke and therefore she too was royal. But the duke was consumed by it. He insisted that people would curtsey to her and call her "Ma'am". My Papa used to say "what's in a curtsey?". But as we know, the royal family took a very hard line on this and refused Mrs Simpson the title. The royal family made it very difficult for people of rank to see the Windsors because of the HRH issue. We saw them fairly often after the war when they came privately to London. My stepmother was on the scene by then and she used to organise the dinners. Actually I was married to Basil and he met David. He liked him.' The whole issue of Wallis's lack of royal status was to colour David's relations with his family until his death. But it was not the only issue.

Valerie is critical of the role of George VI's wife, Queen Elizabeth, (now the Queen Mother). 'I think her attitude to the Windsors was petty. She was simply horrified that the king had abdicated and married a divorced commoner. It meant that her husband had to become king, something they had not been prepared for. She was worried that George was not a healthy man. In fact he was a bit pathetic. She knew that the war was coming and this meant that they'd either have to go to America or stick it out. Queen Elizabeth knew that it would all be a great strain. I think that she blamed George's cancer on the Windsors. I can't believe that – he smoked like a trooper. I'm not a mad fan of the Queen Mother. But they did do their stuff down the East End of London; whenever there was a bomb they went. I don't think they were too displeased when Buckingham Palace was bombed. I don't know who got at George on the HRH business but somebody did.'

Apart from rows over money and the use of royal property, the other contentious area was what exactly David was meant to do with himself. Valerie feels that this was the deepest cut of all. 'It was cruel not to give him a role. Suddenly here he was with literally nothing to do. The war was about to start and he was left feeling that he had nothing valuable to offer. It was awful. He didn't think that abdication would mean that. He had nothing to do. It was all so trivial. Now it was impossible for George to allow David to remain near the front line, but to allow him to be sent to a twopenny-halfpenny island was terrible. Whoever decided to send him as a messenger-boy to the Bahamas? I think that disgusted him. Wallis was far from amused when she saw the governor's house on the island. My father never told me who did what in relation to the arrangements for the Windsors, but it upset him because David never had any sense in the beginning that his exile would be permanent.' Looking back Valerie feels that the whole affair was terribly sad. 'When

I met them after the war I thought he was a sad man. I think she did love him. And I think she did her best to keep him happy. But I think she became difficult as time went on. What had they to do but dress up and go out? Maybe that was enough for her but it wasn't enough for him. In the end they had nothing but each other.'

1 Monckton's account of the abdication quoted in *Walter Monckton: The Life of Viscount Monckton of Brenchley*. Lord Birkenhead, p125.
2 Abdication speech, quoted in *King Edward VIII: The Official Biography*. Phillip Ziegler, p331.
3 *King Edward VIII: The Official Biography*. Phillip Ziegler, p297.
4 *Walter Monckton: The Life of Viscount Monckton of Brenchley*. Lord Birkenhead, p124.
5 Fort Belvedere.
6 *Walter Monckton: The Life of Viscount Monckton of Brenchley*. Lord Birkenhead, p127.
7 Lady Thelma Furness's memoir quoted in *King Edward VIII: The Official Biography*. Phillip Ziegler, p196.
8 *Walter Monckton: The Life of Viscount Monckton of Brenchley*. Lord Birkenhead, pp129, 130.
9 *Ibid*. pp132, 133.
10 *Ibid*. p148.
11 *Ibid*. p152.

3

HAVING A JOLLY GOOD TIME

Court circles as well as the law will be interested in the coming-out of Miss Valerie Monckton, daughter of Mr Walter Monckton, Attorney General to the Duchy of Cornwall, and granddaughter of Sir Thomas Colyer-Fergusson of Ightham Mote.

Miss Monckton, who is very tall and dark, is a fine rider and hunts with the East Kents. She has just finished her education in Paris and with her father has been spending Easter in Cornwall on the Duchy Estate. She will be a debutante at a Buckingham Palace garden reception.[1]

'As I remember it I just had a jolly good time.' Valerie's memories of her teenage years are a whirlwind of fun and excitement. 'I think that there was a sense that everything was about to change; the war was coming so it was a case of enjoy oneself while one can.' Valerie was, perhaps, more conscious of the inevitability of war than many of those taken in by Neville Chamberlain's aggressive appeasement policy, because her father was listening to Winston Churchill's informed warnings about Hitler's plans for Eastern Europe. Although Valerie remembers 1936 as one long party, with the exception of her stint as a royal courier, she does recollect that Churchill advised her that she should join the War Office when she met him at Fort Belvedere during the abdication crisis. But Valerie enjoyed a busy social life before things became serious.

Although owing to the Royal mourning, there will be no formal Courts this year, many debutantes will make curtseys at the Buckingham Palace garden receptions. Among these, I hear, is to be Miss Valerie Monckton, daughter of Mr Walter Monckton, KC and Mrs Monckton, of Fishponds, Sea Chart.[2]

Conversation is as popular as dancing with the 1936 debutantes. Hostesses who have decided on a series of cocktail parties instead of the more formal dances include Mrs Walter Monckton and her aunt Lady Max-Muller. Cambridge undergraduates and barristers were among the young men at Mrs Monckton's party for her daughter Valerie. Her son, Mr Gilbert Monckton, brought some friends down from Cambridge. Sir Thomas Colyer-Fergusson, Mrs Monckton's father, was also present. This hostess and Lady Max-Muller are combining to give another cocktail party at the beginning of June for this debutante.[3]

Valerie was formally presented, not at Buckingham Palace as was the usual thing, but at a specially arranged garden party, because the court was still in mourning following the death of George V. It was at this presentation party that Valerie remembers first seeing Wallis Simpson, standing just a little too near the king for the liking of the royal household. 'The dances for the debutantes were enormous. There were chaperons of course and all the mothers sat around watching who was dancing with whom. After a while my mother actually realised that it was a bit of a waste of time coming to them with me. I didn't have a dance for my coming-out because my parents couldn't afford it. In those days my father still wasn't that well off. But the mothers used to kill themselves having these huge parties which must have cost thousands. They were in places like Belgrave Square, and the dresses alone were often a hundred pounds or more. We had cocktail parties instead, but I remember we often sneaked into big dances that we weren't invited to. Lady Max-Muller, who was my mother's Aunt Wander, helped with the expenses. I remember once she told Mummy that I didn't dress very well and so she bought me a dress. I think it probably hurt my mother but the dress was so lovely that I wore it. Wasn't that naughty? The other thing that Lady Max-Muller did was to invite a party of my friends to lunch. It was great; she arranged it for Quaglino's and there were about twenty people there. Unfortunately Aunt Wander didn't think I was very good at the whole business because before she gave the lunch she told me to make sure that I actually spoke to the people on either side of me.'

Valerie was never short of invitations and remembers that she saw a lot of Gilbert's friends as well as young barristers whom she met through her father. Although she feels that she didn't always have as many dresses as some of her contemporaries, she can't recollect it making the slightest difference to the amount of people she met or the fun she had. 'I couldn't buy the dresses I wanted. Some of the other girls were so beautiful but it didn't alter who my friends were one bit. It never occurred to me to think about class or anything like that. I met mostly barristers and naturally I got on with them very well.'

One of the probable side-benefits of her parents' estrangement was that it gave Valerie more freedom, at an age when many parents were determined not to let their female offspring out of their sight. 'One of the things I enjoyed greatly after leaving school was a trip to Copenhagen. I went on a cargo boat with a friend, Mary Kendell. There was a bit of a row about it. My mother didn't think it was a good idea at all but my father was on my side and we won in the end. We had a great time. All of the Danes we met spoke English. And I remember one occasion when we just danced the whole night away at the Tivoli Gardens. Everyone was in cracking form. If anyone got saucy we would just laugh it off or else tell them to get the hell out of it. On the way over to Copenhagen there was one naughty Irishman who we played poker with, but it was all fun. I don't think many girls would have been allowed to head off on their own like that.'

Valerie's memories of the fun she had during the period before the war are a bit jumbled. Looking back now she just feels it was all one big party. 'There was another trip to Switzerland. I think there were about eight of us. I remember that trip because a boy I had been seeing, a Royal Marine, came along. I'd met him at a dance at Buckingham Palace. I'd gone to the ball with my father, but in those days if the palace was short of young men they'd write to the commanding officer of the regiment and ask for a number of presentable officers. I sat next to Godfrey Pease at this ball, and we got on very well. We had quite a thing for a while. He asked me to marry him on his knees outside our flat on Cadogan Gardens. It was very romantic. My father wasn't so sure. I can't tell what Papa said. It wouldn't be nice. So I said to him – "I'm very fond of you but . . . . " He was very sad. I had several other boyfriends. Never short of them in fact. It was a great time after I left school, with my debs in the middle and the abdication at the end of the year.' Gilbert remembers that he was instrumental in another of Valerie's conquests. 'A great friend of mine at Cambridge, Charlie

Symington, proposed to her. He was very serious. But Valerie didn't want to go to America. So that was that.'

> Miss Valerie Monckton is a debutante who believes in carrying on her voluntary secretarial duties in spite of the social gaieties of the season. Every morning from nine to eleven she goes to her father's chambers in the Temple to see to his correspondence, and again in the late afternoon, when she attends to his outgoing post. Her father, Mr Walter Monckton, is a busy K.C. and Attorney General to the Duchy of Cornwall, as well as Recorder of Hythe.[4]

Valerie recalls that her father frequently told her she should go to as many parties as she liked, but that she should always get up and go to work in the mornings. While even mentioning the possibility that an individual might not get up for work in the morning might sound very odd in the 1990s, this advice was modern, taken in the context of the behaviour of upper-class women in the 1930s. 'One of the things I did before starting work for my father was to go and learn shorthand and typing. Papa wanted me to go to Pitman's but I went to the Monkey Club. It was all very strict. If you went out for a snack at lunchtime you weren't allowed sit with a boy. There was a friend of my brother's on the same course as me and he used to say it was pretty ridiculous. So we ignored the rule and went to the local Lyon's tea house on Kingsway. Well, they noticed and told me that if I did it again I would have to leave. Wasn't that silly?'

Looking back, Valerie admits that fun and the pursuit of it dominated her life between school and the war, but she was not left untouched by the possibility of impending social upheaval, foreshadowed in the Jarrow Marches.

> Humiliated, degraded and intimidated by the Labour Exchanges, the Means Test, the Poor Law and the police, the British Unemployed were a vast malleable force which only needed a leader for it to become a threat. When it marched on London, as it frequently did, like a dark, singing worm, there was an immediate but quite unnecessary tension. The worm, grudgingly allowed its civic rights, would be met and escorted through side-streets if possible to Hyde Park by foot and mounted police, where it would chop itself up into smaller – and safer – pieces and listen to Wal Hannington or Aneurin

Bevan. Occasionally it was entertained by Oswald Mosley and the British Union of Fascists, a predominantly middle-class movement which was big enough on November 1st, 1936, for its leaders to boast that it would put up a hundred candidates at the next general election. But the unemployed remained unbeguiled. The oblique violence inherent in the BUF movement offered nothing to those who had been hurt enough without wishing to hurt others, and as for the BUF's other main ingredient, jingoism, this was quite ludicrously unappealing. So the unemployed resembled a torpid hippo sinking deeper and deeper into the silt left behind by outdated industries and the refuse of a defunct economy.[5]

The Jarrow Marches, more than any other phenomenon, epitomise the deprivation and squalor experienced by Britain's under-class in the 1920s and 1930s. In her book, *The Town That Was Murdered*, Jarrow's MP, 'Red' Ellen Wilkinson, describes the plight of its workers:

> Charles Palmer started Jarrow as a shipbuilding centre without considering the needs of the workers. They crowded into a small colliery village which was hurriedly extended to receive them. They packed into insanitary houses. They lived without social amenities. They paid with their lives for the absence of any preparation for the growth of such a town. And in 1933 another group of capitalists decided the fate of Jarrow without reference to the workers.[6]

By the summer of 1936 Jarrow's townspeople had had enough. Plans were made for a great march on London. Two hundred men were chosen and on 5 October they set out on the three-hundred-mile walk. Their aim was to arrive in London around the time that the new king, Edward VIII, opened Parliament.

> The King's sympathy for the unemployed was well known. What was quite unknown, at least to all these humble, stricken men who had reason to put more faith in princes than politicians, was that this particularly hopeful king would make his first and last journey to Westminster with a heart so filled with his personal anxieties that there would be little room for theirs and only a few more weeks of his reign left to go.[7]

Valerie was at a dance at the Savoy when she first set her eyes on a group of Jarrow marchers. 'The hotel looked out on the Strand and I happened to be near a window, having a drink. I saw this group of bedraggled, pathetic people in terrible clothes and cloth caps. I remember asking someone who they were and afterwards discussing it with my father. I thought to myself – aren't I lucky? Drinking champagne, dancing with lovely people and having a great time. By comparison with these unfortunates we were so well-off. One could only be uncomfortable. It really hit me. It was a turning point. It made me think. But of course I wasn't political at all. So there was no sense in me attacking the system or anything. I was conscious of poverty because I had often heard my father talking with his friends, but it would never have occurred to me to question the idea of having servants. But just thinking as I did would separate me from people. I remember being put down by one young man when I mentioned my concern for the Jarrow people and the poverty that was obvious at the time. He said to me "Good gracious! You must be one of these philosophical types. Let's get on with the dancing." I was surprised that anyone who had seen the marchers could react like that. But they did.

'Gilbert was very keen on my joining the First Aid Nursing Yeomanry or FANY's, as they were known. He had been in the Territorials while in Cambridge and had gone straight into the Enniskillen Dragoon Guards after university. Because we were living near Sloane Street, he suggested that I should join up at the Duke of York Barracks there.' The FANY's had an honourable record and had won distinction and praise for their work in the First World War. 'As far back as the Boer War these women had gone out on horseback to care for the wounded. I can't remember exactly when I joined, but Gilbert was always urging me to get involved. When I did, I went twice a week, as I remember, between six and seven at night. We would do two or three hours' training with the Red Cross. There was one woman in particular who I remember. She talked to us one night about her experience in the First World War when she was an ambulance driver. What she said brought the reality of what it was all about home to me. She talked about what it would be like in a real war and how the men would be in a mess by the time we got to them as nurses. She talked about what she had seen and the horror of it all. Before that we had been marching up and down and enjoying it all. There was a lot of dressing up and going to camp but what she said made us stop and think.' So although she was having a 'jolly good time', Valerie had been stopped in her tracks and made to pause and reflect.

Another thought-provoking event had occurred in Fort Belvedere, when Winston Churchill warned her that war was imminent. In the late 1930s Churchill stood virtually alone in his opposition to Neville Chamberlain and the appeasers. He had long supported a strong defence policy and had been isolated and excluded from office because of his passionate belief that the evil stirrings in central Europe should be resisted:

> There can be little doubt that Chamberlain was the choice not only of Conservative MPs but of the general public, and that Churchill was seen as a scaremonger. Sir John Reith saw to it that he was seldom heard over the BBC, and in that Reith had the full backing of the prime minister . . . . The voices of 1930s appeasement fall strangely on the ear today; at the time a consensus of Englishmen not only thought them sensible, but those who argued otherwise were scorned, vilified and even accused of treason.[8]

Valerie listened to Churchill and heard what he was saying. He suggested that she should try and join the War Office. 'It seemed like a good idea and I knew that my father agreed with a lot of what Churchill was saying. In the end I didn't go into the War Office until after Chamberlain's infamous "peace in our time" speech when he came back from Munich in September 1938. After that it was obvious that war was inevitable. I got a call from a senior woman in the FANY's who asked me join the new Auxiliary Territorial Service. They were looking for younger women, and I was told that I would be a sergeant. My first job was at St George's Hospital, half of which they had turned into a recruiting office. I don't think I was great at that. There was a lot of filling in of forms. Not me at all.'

Valerie has always admired Winston Churchill and remembers cursing those who had ignored his warnings about the dangers of appeasement and the idiocy of disarmament as he saw it. 'If the war had started then, in 1938, England would have been in trouble. We weren't ready. That year was very important for the preparation.' During her period in the War Office Valerie worked on a reconnaissance operation. 'We worked from a tiny flat in London with no name plate or anything to identify the building as belonging to the military. We didn't have uniforms and the whole business was done very quietly. There were about eight of us and we worked to a brigadier. Our job was to locate suitable sites for anti-aircraft guns as well as the searchlights. We worked mainly on the east coast in teams. Afterwards we would drive back to the flat in London and draw up the map locations.'

Although 1939 is often described as the year in which the lights went out all over Europe, for Valerie it was also the year in which she met and married Sir Basil Goulding. 'Gilbert was going out with a girl called Mary Lillis at the time. Her brother, Barry, was at college with him. They were all coming to Ireland for the races at Fairyhouse that Easter. There was going to be lots of dances and parties. Maybe Gilbert had quarrelled with his girlfriend, I'm not sure, but he invited me to come with him. So I got a couple of days' leave from the War Office and travelled over. Then during the racing there was a dinner in somebody's house, Barry's I think, and it turned out that I was seated next to Basil. There were about sixteen people at the dinner and later there was a dance at the Gresham Hotel in Dublin. Of course I knew no one. I remember thinking that this fellow next to me was rather nice. I told him straight away that I knew nothing about racing and he said "neither do I but my father went mad on it". We got on very well. Then he said that he had his car outside and that he would take me to the Gresham. So I went with him and it was great fun. Very noisy and lots of streamers, but not great for talking.

'When we got back it was very late and he asked me if I was staying another day to race on the Monday. I explained about having to get back for work. He really wanted me to stay so I said that maybe I would win on the horses and then I could fly back to England. So I stayed and the next day I put a bet on and won ten pounds. Basil drove me to Baldonnel for the plane. Unfortunately after the goodbyes and the parting it ran out of petrol and we had to turn back. I was in a terrible state because I knew that I would be a day late. In the end I got back to work on the Wednesday. But though I hadn't wanted to be late, it didn't matter because it was clear straight away that we had clicked. Before I left Baldonnel he had asked me to get more leave and come and meet his mother in Ireland. I was hooked so I promised that I would. I remember he said, "you may see me sooner than you think". Later that night when I got back, he rang me. My mother took the call and wanted to know who this Irishman was. I hadn't noticed that he sounded Irish until I heard him on the telephone. The whole trip seemed like one long ball. He was a terrific dancer and he was so handsome. He was very dark and had blue eyes though he wasn't that tall. But he was hugely entertaining, so good looking, enormously attractive and he spoke so well.' In true Mills and Boon style Valerie had fallen in love. 'I was very physically attracted to Basil and I wanted to get married straight away.' And they did.

Sir William Lingard Amphlett, Basil's father, died in 1935, four years before Valerie met Basil:

> The death has occurred in London on June 20 of Sir William Lingard Amphlett Goulding, Bart, of Hillbrook, Castleknock, Co. Dublin. While on his way to Ascot he was taken suddenly ill on the train, and was hurried to a hospital, where an immediate operation was performed. A second operation on Thursday unfortunately had fatal consequences.
>
> Sir Lingard Goulding was prominently identified with the industrial and commercial life of this country, and was connected with many important concerns.
>
> The only son of the first baronet, the Right Hon Sir Joshua Goulding, PC, DL, JP, and Ada, only daughter of the late Charles Lingard Stokes, of Pauntley, Worcestershire, England, he was born on the 5th of October, 1883. He succeeded his father in 1925. In the year 1908 he married Nesta Violet, second daughter of the Hon Mr Justice George Wright, of the High Court of Justice in Ireland, and granddaughter of Sir Croker Barrington of Glenstal, County Limerick. During the Great War he served as a lieutenant in the South of Ireland Imperial Yeomanry, and later as captain in the 1st Battalion Royal Irish Fusiliers.
>
> Later he entered business life, and became chairman of W and H M Goulding Ltd, of Dublin, and also a director of the Great Northern Railway (Ireland) Ltd. He was, in addition, a director of a number of important companies, including Metropolitan Vickers Electrical Company Ltd, Imperial Smelting Corporation, and Messrs E and J Burke Ltd, and the North British and Mercantile Insurance Company's local Board. One of his most important directorships, however, was that of the Bank of Ireland, of which he was elected Governor in 1932.
>
> Deceased was even better known, perhaps, in the world of sport than in the field of business, and it was very seldom indeed that he failed to attend

race meetings in the Phoenix Park, at Leopardstown, or the Curragh, while it was a point of honour with him that he should not miss the great English events like the Derby and the Grand National. He had a number of horses in training with Mr Maxwell Arnott, of Greenmount, Clonsilla.

He was a good polo player and for many years was associated with the All-Ireland Polo Club, for which he played regularly up to about two years ago.

The title is inherited by Mr Basil Goulding, his eldest son, who, at a very early age, already has shown himself to be an unusually competent business man. Mr Basil Goulding was born in 1909, and Sir Lingard's second son, Ossian, was born in 1913.[9]

According to Goulding family lore the late Sir William Lingard died as he had lived, shouting 'Bugger, it's Ascot tomorrow' as he lay dying. In an appreciation Viscount Castlerosse, the eccentric bon viveur and son of the 5th Earl of Kenmare, wrote:

> Truly Lingard Goulding was a shining mark. His public life is well known. He was a most successful Governor of the Bank of Ireland during a most difficult time, but rather would I lay stress on his personal attributes, for he was an altogether delightful companion. Often when he came over here did I revel in his wit and gaiety, and besides he was always well informed. He loved horses and the country life with gusto. His home was in Dublin, where his business was too. We can ill spare this level-headed lovable man.[10]

By the time Valerie met Basil, he had inherited his father's title and was living with his recently remarried mother, the beautiful Nesta Violet, in Castleknock in County Dublin. Sir Basil was thirty years of age and had been chairman of the family's fertiliser business since his father's death in 1935. By all accounts Basil was regarded as a good catch. He had been engaged, but the affair had ended. It is clear, however, that his bachelor status was a cause of worry to his uncle and godfather, Edward Goulding, otherwise Lord Wargrave, the influential Tory and chairman of Rolls Royce.

Shiplake Court
Henley-On-Thames
Sept 29th 1934

My dear Basil,
Many thanks for your newsy letter, which I thoroughly enjoyed. I hope to see you here for a night when over as there are one or two matters I want to chat

49

with you. I have altered my will materially in your favour also I am prepared to transfer to you some more stock this year – I hope that before very long I may hear that you have met the lady that is going to share your lot in life – I am getting old and will reach my 72nd year this November.[11]

Lord Wargrave took a huge interest in his nephew, and treated Basil like the son he never had himself. While Basil was at Oxford in the late 1920s and early 1930s, Wargrave wrote to him regularly and took a keen interest in Basil's very successful and varied sporting activities. The correspondence also shows that Basil's uncle 'Paddy', as Wargrave was known, looked after his nephew's financial affairs, advising on share purchase as well as making substantial monetary gifts on a regular basis. A great sense of affection and warmth pervades the letters exchanged between Basil and his uncle, as well as some indication that perhaps Basil was closer to Wargrave than he was to his father:

> My dear Basil,
>
> I am very sorry for you and your news. It is quite certain if there is any doubt in the matter you are right to take action now and not when it is too late. There are too many cases of unhappiness not rectified until too late. I hope that things will right in your interest and for your happiness. I have destroyed your letter . . . better luck dear Basil and may the ultimate decision evolve in your good luck and happiness.
>
> Your affectionate uncle Ted.[12]

Wargrave's concern for Basil's personal happiness is evident throughout the letters, as is his obvious interest in drawing Basil into the 'right' circles in Britain. Uncle Paddy was in a very good position to help the young Basil:

> Paddy Goulding was a tall, thin, genial figure, a wealthy Anglo-Irishman (his father had been MP for Cork) educated at Cambridge. He had been in Parliament almost continuously since 1895 and, as a passionate admirer of Joseph Chamberlain, was entirely committed to imperialism and social reform. He was a founder member of the Tariff Reform League, and had been chairman of its Organization Department since 1904. Chamberlain called him the best organizer he had ever known, and J L Garvin, the editor of the *Observer*, described him as 'a legend behind the scenes and a power in

politics without being either a minister or a force in debate . . . . There never was a more potent backbencher in the House of Commons; nor a surer, shrewder manager of human nature in the lobbies and the dining room'.[13]

Wargrave was a bachelor and enjoyed entertaining. His sister acted as hostess at his house, Wargrave Hall, and later at Shiplake Court where he gave weekend parties and dinners. He was close to many politicians, including F E Smith, Andrew Bonar Law and Sir Edward Carson. Paddy was also on very good terms with Max Aitken, later Lord Beaverbrook, who put him on the board of Rolls Royce after he acquired it in 1910. Aitken, who was to follow Lord Northcliffe as Britain's biggest press baron, acknowledged his debt to Wargrave, whom he regarded as having encouraged his political career when he was little more than a wide-boy fresh over from his native Canada. 'In politics I am the product of your encouragement. You had the foresight to know that I could do something.'[14]

Typical of Wargrave's efforts on Basil's behalf is an invitation sent to Basil while he was still at Oxford in 1931, to join Max Aitken and himself for dinner at Goldsmiths' Hall, a London club: 'You and Max Aitken both dine with me at top table and I'll stand you your expenses. White tie, waistcoat and tail coat – your affectionate uncle.'[15] As his university days neared an end, it appears that Basil was coming under pressure from both his father and uncle to decide on a career. Writing back to Basil after what appears to have been a successful dinner at Goldsmiths', Wargrave mentions his nephew's desire to become an architect, a career choice not favoured by the family:

> Thank you for your nice letter. I am glad that you enjoyed the dinner and also that you liked Max [Aitken] . . . . You are quite right to think calmly over the Goulding proposition – no doubt your Dad would much like to have you with him and there are certain obvious openings. I never was keen on architecture as a profit making concern – but if – in England I ought to be able to help you to some Boards but that will become more and more difficult as these times we live in . . . you must rightly make the decision yourself. All good luck and with affectionate interest, your godfather and uncle.[16]

In later years Basil would always describe himself as a spoiled architect. Shortly after leaving Oxford, he bowed to the inevitable draw of the business world, taking a diploma of merit at the London School of Accountancy. But life was good for this young and well-connected future baronet. June 1935 saw him driving across America with a pal *en route* from the motor racing at Indianapolis, from where he wrote a long, descriptive letter to his mother, 'Jum':

> The race at Indianapolis was a spectacle rather than a thrill. There were three killed in practice and one more in the race, and a couple others were as lucky as cats not to be, so that presumably some people were thrilled. But none of this incident happened opposite our stand or on the corner to right of it. However we were right opposite the pits and saw all the queer cars very closely and took pictures of them which should be good. And the crowd of 160,000 made good screaming. It was an original event to us and well worth seeing . . . .
>
> My week with Denis in Philadelphia was splendidly varied: he's a wonderful fella to stay with and took a whole lot of trouble to show me all around. We went to races, a horse-show, a slap-up dance and dinner, a very drunken one, a couple of flicks, a couple of lunches, a first night of an Earl Carrol production going on to New York, a very low 'Burlesque' show (which has a special meaning here and is just a startlingly low sort of vaudeville with chorus girls of great shape and the minimum of camouflage to it, comedians far lower than Flanagan and Allen, an almost entirely male audience) – some tennis, some racquets, and some cocktail parties . . . .
>
> They have a good string of Hunt Club dances and private dances, and these are where they put on speed. At the hunt club dance and dinner to which I went about seventy per cent of the guests were soaked by 2 o'clock and it eventually petered out through one half having been wheeled home and the remainder having given up aspirations to dancing. Quite a few had gone off in the garden with each other's girls by then so there was a good deal of dissension and damm-well-going-home-without-her. Denis was unfortunately trying to smooth out one of these situations so we could not get going home ourselves until the odd pair had been retrieved from under an arbutus bush in the paddock. The people don't seem to get roaring or offensively drunk I must say – they are too practised for that – they just get preserved like fishing bait in a spirits bottle.[17]

Basil appears to have had a good relationship with his mother, who must have enjoyed her son's missive from America. Later in the same letter, he talks openly about his attempts to place himself next to the 'choicest thing I could see at dinner' and of his thwarted attempts to land a native female companion. On his twenty-first birthday, while he was still at Oxford, 'Jum' wrote to him in the most loving terms: 'I can't help congratulating myself too on Nov. 4th which is the best day I ever had or shall have in my existence because of what it brought me! Thank you so very much for being you.' Valerie remembers that she was initially terrified of Basil's mother. 'It was the most frightening time in my life. Basil had lived with his mother at Hillbrook after his father died. He died while Basil was in America in 1935. I just thought that it was odd that he lived with her at his age. Thank heavens she got married again just before I met him because from what I had heard she had never liked his previous girlfriends. He had been engaged to a very nice girl but he broke it off. I felt very sorry for her. I think it was a bit of a *cause célèbre*.'

Basil not only rang Valerie on the night after she returned to London following their first meeting, but he set about making arrangements to see her there. Both Walter and Polly liked Basil when they met him, and more importantly let Valerie know that they did. They became engaged on her second visit to Ireland. 'We were in Wicklow near the Sallygap. Basil suggested that we walk around the lake. And then he asked me to marry him. I told him that I wanted to, but explained how I felt awful about leaving my mother and father. I thought that my going might cause the end of the marriage altogether. I felt that I was the only one between them. He just said "I'll give you one day". Basil was very serious. He wasn't making any jokes that day. He just said to me "it's your life". I felt as if I was being pulled in two directions. I felt this awful responsibility. My brother was away so I felt it was all on me. At the time my father wasn't involved with anyone else so they were sort of together – in the same house at least. In the end I knew that I had done all I could. After all, I had made him give up one woman. The war was coming and I knew that I had to take my chance as well. Once I made up my mind I enjoyed it.'

The Daily Herald regarded news of the impending engagement important enough to put on its front page under the headline 'KC's Daughter to Marry'.[18] Basil's mother was thrilled by the news and wrote to him from London:

> I think Valerie is a splendid girl and so interesting, I have the brightest hopes
> for your happiness . . . you deserve it if anyone ever did. You can't think what
> a joy and relief to my mind it is that you won't be alone at Hillbrook anymore.
> I may tell you (and of course you knew it) that I was fretting considerably
> over having left you although I hid it quite well from Stanley and (perhaps ?)
> from you, now I feel the utmost happiness in the thought of you both at
> Hillbrook and it will be such fun for you planning it all out with her and fixing
> it up. Would the ruby ring suit her a treat?[19]

Nesta's letter is full of excitement and of keeping the news 'hush hush'
until Basil and Valerie travelled to London to meet her parents, when
the engagement would be official. Sir Walter Monckton's telegram
dated 17 July was preserved in Sir Basil's papers. He 'was delighted to
see' Basil and told him to ring as soon as he got to London so that they
could arrange a meeting.

With all the formalities out of the way, Basil and Valerie set about
enjoying the last summer before the outbreak of war. In August they
headed for Donegal, where they joined some of Basil's friends who
were holidaying there. Before they left, Basil received a letter of
congratulations from his friend Pride who was soldiering in Calcutta.
Had Valerie seen it she would have had an interesting insight into how
some men talk about women behind their backs.

> Old cock you have provided me with my first genuine piece of excitement
> for a rare long time and I feel as if I were at least partly engaged myself. Your
> telegram arrived in the office this morning and fair woke me up. The first
> seven words very nearly gave me a stroke, life or death practically depending
> on the name to follow. You will be hideously busy and preoccupied but in due
> course I really must have a report illustrated with diagram on the following
> lines 1: pulchritude: in great detail not omitting colour, size, shape of each
> working part and state of repair. 2: Age. 3: Breeding. 4: Intelligence. 5: Wit.
> 6: Whether educated or illiterate variety. 7: Can she see a Hillbrook john? 8:
> I hope she's bad at golf. 9: Is the leather on her Ⓓ well polished by saddle
> or is that foreign to her? 10: Is she a nice mover. 11: Has she an eye for
> reasonable clothes – or did you win her with your sample coat? If so you'll
> have striped children. 12: Can she sing, play the mouth-organ, screw a nut,
> play bicycle polo, tolerate Ireland, tolerate cad's motor cars, do home nursing,
> run a house, run a garden, choose a reasonable curtain or bedspread?
> 13: Finally what must I keep from her?[20]

No record remains of Sir Basil's reply.

Valerie loved Donegal. Part of the holiday was spent with the Porters, who had a house near Downings. The emphasis was on outdoor activities: they camped, played tennis, swam and walked with a changing group of people, including Cecil and Betty Hodson, who became lifelong friends. But while Valerie enjoyed herself in a remote part of the north-west of Ireland, the London gossip columnists were spreading the news of her wedding plans :

> An interesting addition to the already important list of September brides is Miss Valerie Monckton, daughter of Sir Walter Monckton, Attorney General to the Duchy of Cornwall and Lady Monckton, whose engagement to Sir Basil Goulding was announced recently. Lady Monckton tells me that her daughter has now decided on her wedding date. It is to be on Wednesday, Sept. 20, at the Temple Church. Her father's association with the Temple as a Bencher of the Inner Temple is the reason for the bride's choice of this church. After the ceremony bride and bridegroom and their guests will walk across to the Inner Temple Hall, where the reception will be held.[21]

Six bridesmaids had been picked and the dressmaking operation was well in hand. One of the bridesmaids, Basil's cousin Fay, wrote saying how much she was looking forward to the wedding: 'the dresses sound wonderful and it is too good of you and Auntie Nesta to give me mine as a Christmas present'.[22] With all the telegrams and letters of congratulations and goodwill they were receiving it must have appeared to Basil and Valerie that the whole world was united in celebrating their happiness. Seeing the announcement in the newspaper, Basil's first nurse, a Mrs O'Leary, wrote saying that she sent the 'best of good wishes for your engagement to be married soon as you were always a good child to me'.[23]

In fact by the time Mrs O'Leary wrote her letter Basil and Valerie were already married, in a ceremony not at all like the one planned by their enthusiastic families. 'With the announcement of the war only weeks away I got a telegram that was redirected to Donegal telling me that I had been called up. I was in an awful state. I was, after all, a quarter trained. I was an ATS sergeant. I felt it was my duty to go. The telegram instructed me to report to Guildford training camp. Basil didn't want me to go, so I sent a sort of delaying letter saying where I was. Basil wanted us to get married straight away because as a married woman I would be exempted. I took about a fortnight to make up my mind, and in the end we decided to get married there and then in Downings. But when we went to see the local vicar he told us that as I was still not twenty-one, we would have to see a bishop. But we couldn't find one. It was terrible. Eventually we found out that there was a bishop about but he was playing golf. Once we found him he told us to get my father's consent. That was an agonising moment because Papa could have been anywhere. He was in the Ministry of Information by then and I was worried that we wouldn't be able to catch up with him. But we did. He telegraphed back and told us to to get married at once. I was delighted: I knew that he had liked Basil. So instead of this grand London wedding we had a short ceremony with hardly anyone there. I remember on the morning I just cried in the lavatory.'

> It was announced in London today that because of the crisis, the marriage of Sir William Basil Goulding and Miss Valerie Hamilton Monckton, daughter of Sir Walter Monckton, KC arranged for September 20 has taken place quietly at Holy Trinity Church, Carrigart, County Donegal.[24]

'As I remember it the vicar's name was Canon Dowse. There was nobody belonging to me there. My mother would have come but my brother was about to be mobilised and so she wanted to be with him. I think there were about eight people at the wedding. A couple called the Milnes, the Porters, some other people and Basil and I. Lady Milne, whom we didn't know at all, gave me a ring. She was so kind. There was no music, singing or anything like that. I was wearing an ordinary old skirt and Basil had his coat of many colours. I don't suppose it could have been called a joyful ceremony. And as far as I remember we got into the car and drove to Dublin straight afterwards. When we got to Basil's house in Castleknock it was all shut up, and who was on the step only Basil's three-year-old niece with a card around her neck saying who she was and that she was destined for Canada and her grandmother. Ossian, Basil's brother, wanted to get her out of Europe with the war starting. Poor little thing. We had to sort her out before we could celebrate our wedding. After that we were still left with a house that

contd. p73

Valerie aged about fourteen.

Valerie and Polly at Chateau d'Oeux in Switzerland. Polly took Gilbert to Switzerland to help cure his TB.

Valerie's father, Viscount Monckton of Brenchley.

Gwendolen Yelf, Valerie's beloved nanny, pictured here with Lingard. Valerie asked 'Nanny' to come and help when Lingard was born in the summer of 1940. This picture was taken at Egham – Valerie and Basil's first real home in England.

Valerie's mother and father, Polly and Walter, pose outside their home, Fishponds, with Valerie,
her dog 'Trousers' and brother Gilbert.

Gilbert at Fishponds while on holiday from Harrow.

Valerie when she was about eight years of age with her dog 'Trousers', at her grandfather's home at Ightham Mote in Kent.

Valerie and her dog 'Pericles' at Dargle Lodge.

Valerie's mother 'Polly' at Dargle.

Valerie in business mode.

Valerie on leave wearing her ATS uniform outside The Barley Mow pub in Egham, London.

Sir Basil Goulding's mother, Nesta Violet. Affectionately called 'Jum', she married Stanley Adams of Thomas Cook Travel after her first husband died.

Basil and Valerie on a 'bicycle made for two' in Holland.

*Basil and Valerie in Donegal before their
wedding in August 1939.*

Valerie at the races.

Basil and Valerie riding at Hillbrook in Castleknock, County Dublin, not long after their marriage.

Valerie holidaying in Sicily.

Valerie on a camping holiday with her friend Betty Hodson.

Tim and Ham as pages at a family wedding in London.

Ham gets a firm hand at a London wedding.

Valerie and Basil's children, Lingard, Tim and Ham, on the spiral staircase at Dargle.

Basil, Valerie, Tim and Ham at the same wedding.

Valerie was not pleased when 'the boys' produced this photograph after she asked them to have a 'proper' picture taken of the three of them.

A portrait of 'the boys' taken at Dargle.

The family photographed in front of a painting of Basil's grandfather by William Orpen.

Valerie photographed at Dargle before going to a 'do'.

Valerie resting during a skiing holiday.

Basil loved dogs as much as Valerie. He is seen here with 'Bunter'.

Basil was a first-class skier. Val D'Isère 1960.

Basil and Valerie in Montreal for St Patrick's Day.

contd. from p56

was closed up and no honeymoon in sight. So Basil rang the Hodsons who lived in Templeogue and asked if we could stay. Well, Betty put down the telephone and we could hear her saying to Cecil "here's the invitation to the wedding in London on September 20th. What's going on?". I think they thought we were jumping the gun a bit. But they said to come and stay with them. And when we got there they had white ribbons on the gateway and they had champagne ready. They really made it for us. We even had their bedroom.'

In retrospect, Valerie thinks that people must have been surprised by their rapid nuptials. 'I was English. I had never been to Ireland before I met Basil. I don't suppose they found me very interesting and I think that some of Basil's circle were furious with me for taking a bachelor they all wanted. But Basil and I had clicked straight away. In those days I was fairly good-looking and I didn't talk horses permanently like some girls did. I laughed at his jokes, which I think pleased him. Others didn't always understand Basil's humour but I did. We talked and he was relaxed with me and our conversation flowed. We were easy.' Valerie says that they 'kissed quite a good bit' but they didn't do anything that wasn't 'proper' until after they were married. 'I remember when we were camping, Betty Hodson used to come into the tent and remind us that we weren't married yet. We did enjoy each other very much. When we did try to make love I wasn't able. I was too small and Basil was so wonderful about it. It could have been terrible but he was very kind. It didn't take long to sort it out. We went to a gynaecologist while we were staying with the Hodsons. It was only a small procedure and we had no problems at all after that. Of course I knew nothing about having babies, nothing about contraception. Basil had said that he didn't want children but I told him that I wanted a child in case he was killed in the war. I wanted a child to remember him by. In fact I was expecting within a month of our first making love. I think he was surprised that it all happened so quickly.'

---

1 From an undated newspaper cutting in Lady Goulding's possession.
2 *Ibid.*
3 *Ibid.*
4 *Ibid.*

5 *The Age of Illusion*. Ronald Blythe. Oxford University Press, London 1983, p156.

6 *Ibid*. pp163, 164.

7 *Ibid*. p166.

8 *The Caged Lion: Sir Winston Spencer Churchill 1932–1940*. William Manchester. Abacus, London 1992, p245.

9 From a press cutting in Lady Goulding's possession.

10 *Ibid*.

11 Lord Wargrave to Sir Basil Goulding, dated 29 September; the year is calculated as 1934.

12 *Ibid*. 20 August; year omitted.

13 *Beaverbrook: A Life*. Anne Chisholm and Michael Davie. Pimlico, London 1993.

14 *Ibid*. p74.

15 Lord Wargrave to Sir Basil Goulding, 17 January 1931.

16 *Ibid*. 24 January 1931.

17 Basil Goulding to his mother who was called 'Jum', 1 June 1935.

18 *The Daily Herald*, 20 July 1939.

19 Nesta Violet to Basil, 15 July 1939.

20 To Basil from his friend Pride, 21 July 1939.

21 *The Daily Telegraph* and *Morning Post*, 23 August 1939.

22 Cousin Fay to Basil, 13 August 1939.

23 Mrs O'Leary to Basil, 1 September 1939.

24 *Evening Standard*, 30 September 1939.

4

DOING HER BIT

There is a certain sense of loneliness in Valerie's recollection of the year she spent at Hillbrook following her marriage. *Tatler* magazine gave a whole page of pictures to the newly-weds in its 11 October edition. In one picture, 'Lady Goulding does a job of work, labour being a bit difficult': in another photograph, Basil and Valerie are sitting on 'Mo-Bikes' because, as the caption explains, they use less petrol (it had just been rationed). The house itself, photographed in sepia tones, shows a large square, ivy-clad structure with two ample bay windows facing onto a rockery leading down to parkland and trees. Three dormer windows and five shuttered front bedroom windows connive to create an almost continental effect. The 'happy couple' were photographed in a very formal pose, which created an image of the untouchable, the aristocratic and the aloof: not at all like Valerie's image of herself.

Tatler's portrait is in direct contrast to Valerie's own memories of the period. 'I did absolutely nothing all day. There were four sisters, the Hamiltons, who used to ask me to tea and the vicar used to ask me to do things, but I thought that because I was pregnant that I should do nothing. I used to walk my four miles or whatever but that was it. I was so terrified of losing the baby that I did nothing. Basil was in the Goulding's office in Molesworth Street and I would be at home in Castleknock. There was a cook, housemaid, parlour-maid, gardener and groom, so there was nothing for me to do.' Whether or not Valerie was kept at a distance by some of Basil's circle is impossible to validate now, but one thing is sure: she felt alone. 'The only person I spoke to was Willie Kerrigan, the groom. In fact there wasn't any riding at Castleknock before I came, because although Basil's father rode, Basil only took it up later to please me. Lingard had been a great polo player and Willie had been all over the place with him playing polo. He

75

travelled to Argentina with him when the Irish polo team played out there. I used to talk to Willie quite a bit. He was my friend at that time.'

Valerie would often claim that she was more comfortable with people from outside her social class and milieu; a facility she would later use to great effect when soliciting funds for the clinic in the Dublin cattle market or Moore Street. Valerie remembers feeling that Willie's living conditions at Castleknock were not what they should have been: 'Willie and the family lived in an extraordinary state. I can't remember how many children they had but there wasn't enough room for all of them. They lived in this very cramped place above the stables. It seemed awful to me but I didn't say anything to Basil because he had grown up with it.' The fact that Valerie said nothing probably highlights the nature of their relationship at that early stage of their marriage: she was almost ten years younger than her husband, had known him barely four months when she married him, and was an outsider on his patch.

Valerie's sojourn at Hillbrook was short. Although they had married precipitately in order to avoid Valerie's call-up, Basil was determined that he would 'do his bit'. 'Basil wanted to join the Irish army. Like many people, he hoped that Ireland would join the war. We knew many Irish people who joined the Irish army thinking that Ireland would join the Allies. But they didn't, so Basil started writing letters. I even wrote to my commanding officer from the War Office and asked if they'd take Basil in the artillery end of things. Early on, the RAF said that he was too old to fly. Later on they started taking older people and that was how he got in. In the meantime he was running the ARP in Dublin. At the beginning of August he got a letter saying that he had been given a commission as a pilot officer in the administrative and special duties branch of the Royal Air Force volunteer reserve. He was told to present himself for immediate service at an officers' training school at Loughborough in Leicestershire. Well, that made things a bit difficult because I had thought that the baby would be born earlier than he was. The problem was that in those days you had to apply to travel to England and if you went you had to stay. So that meant that I had to bring Lingard, who had only been born on 11 July.

'The labour seemed to last for ever, it took three days. He was big – ten and a half pounds – and I was small. I remember the doctor asking me to stick it out because you didn't get many drugs then. It wasn't great and when I tried to breastfeed him that was no good either, which is a bit odd because if you look at me you'd think I could feed dozens. But the thing was that he looked quite normal when he was born because of his size. He was quite healthy at first. But then he got the whooping cough when he was about a year and a half. That was the start of the asthma. So in any case, there I was with a four-week-old baby, not having a clue, on my way to England. The nurse who came home with me after I left the nursing home on Harcourt Street felt really sorry for me. So sorry, that she dosed Lingard with whiskey before we went on board the boat for Holyhead. Men did nothing where babies were concerned then but Basil said he would change its nappies on the boat. And to be fair he did: it was a major effort, but he tried. I remember that when we eventually got to London I ran straight into the Ministry of Information and dumped Lingard in my father's in-tray. The first thing I did when I got to my mother's house was to telegram for my old nanny, Gwendolen Yelf. As far as I remember she came almost immediately.'

Valerie and Basil arrived in Britain at the height of Germany's bombing raids on the south east of England. By 7 September, Hitler had realised that invading Britain was not going to be as easy as he had anticipated, so he diverted the *Luftwaffe's* attention to the destruction of the nation's spirit instead: the bombing of London began.[1] 'Basil went off to training school and myself and Lingard stayed with my mother who was driving ambulances. We spent a lot of time in the bomb shelters. One day sitting in the shelter during a raid, I got talking to a lady who was obviously very sorry for me because of the baby being so young. There and then she offered me the loan of a house in Oxford. It was amazing. People did things like that during the war. I can't even remember exactly where it was, but it meant that I was able to send Nanny and the baby to this house. I was delighted because I just wanted to be as close to Basil as I could be. I was so much in love that all I could think of was being with him. Around then, Basil was sent to the staff college at Oxford and I joined the Red Cross. They were very helpful in organising accommodation for us. We got one little room with an iron bedstead. Then when it looked like Basil was going to be there for a while, we organised a little house. So Lingard and Nanny came and joined us and we all settled down. As soon as we had done that, Basil was sent as a railway transport officer to Andover.'

Basil was on the move in more ways than one. On 20 January 1940 he was notified of his promotion from pilot officer to flying officer. On 31 January he was made a flight lieutenant and the following June he was made a squadron leader. By the end of 1942 Basil had reached the rank of wing commander and was issued a defence medal at the end of hostilities, for his services.[2] 'Basil didn't like Andover that much. The poor man knew nothing about English railways, not to mention the fact that he didn't know the names of the stations. He was quite a few months at that but it wasn't his *métier*. Of course we all moved again. We got three rooms in a farmhouse. The great thing was that the Red Cross allowed people to move around so I was able to "do my bit" and still follow Basil. It was while we were in Andover that I bought an old ambulance and did it up and put the Irish crest on the side. I wasn't on duty on the day it was driven to London, so I was very cross that I wasn't there for its send-off after all the work I had put in. Then the next move was when Basil was transferred to look after the US planes and their crews. I think somebody realised that he wasn't getting to grips with the railways.

'He enjoyed the new job a lot. His HQ was the RAF in London but the job meant a lot of travelling around various air bases. We had a big problem finding a house, but we eventually got a room in a nice house in Maidenhead. Lingard had the whooping cough at the time so he and Nanny stayed in the room, and myself and Basil stayed in a caravan, in a field near the house. It was either a case of being boiled alive and asphyxiated or else freezing to death. It was then that I went back to the War Office because the Red Cross didn't need me in Maidenhead. All I was doing was filling in ledgers. That meant that I was up and down by train to Nanny and Lingard while Basil went all over the country. Then we heard that there was a possibility that he would be posted to the Middle East, so I decided that if there was a chance that he would be away that I might as well join up. So I joined the army as a private; my number was 350.' In the end, Basil avoided the threat of an overseas posting because of the golfer Henry Cotton, who was determined that he was not going to volunteer. Basil and Valerie had become friendly with the Cottons when the two men were posted together. Cotton decided that if the commanding officer asked for men to volunteer by going through the list alphabetically, he would decline when his name was called. Cotton hoped that because his name would be called out early on, that he might encourage others to say no. One way or another Basil did not have to go to the Middle East but Valerie did 'do her bit'.

'Even though I had been in the ATS before the war began, I had to start at the beginning again when I rejoined. I went for a six-week stint at a training camp near Guildford. That six weeks of initial training was important because it determined your future: whether you were to get NCO or officer training. In the end I passed out, number one in my group. I was very lucky.' Valerie's main recollection of this period is of the many lonely and unhappy girls who just could not cope with the roughness of army life. 'Many of the girls at Guildford were miserable. Many were from Wales and some of them had never left the small mining villages where they were born. Three of us had been to public school. If you have survived boarding school you can put up with anything. So I had no problem at all, but for many of these girls life in camp was very tough. The washing facilities were minimal and we slept in Nissan huts – forty of us to a hut. The loos were awful, no privacy, all together, and the showers were outside in the open. Most of them ignored me at first. Some didn't like me because I was married and had a funny accent. And of course, though I was only twenty-two or twenty-three, they thought of me as old. Maybe also it annoyed some of them that I wasn't put out by the conditions, that I could cope. I felt very sorry for them because they were weeping at night. Some had never been away from their families. I suppose class was the issue.'

Valerie's position had not been made easier by the arrival of letters marked 'Lady'. 'I had asked my mother not to put "Lady" on the envelope because I knew it would cause problems, but she forgot. The result was that the corporal over my group put me in charge of cleaning the toilets. I think she thought it was funny to have a "Lady" sluicing out the loos. But I really didn't mind. I got over their attitude to me with a bit of help from my brother Gilbert. He advised me to let them see that I could be one of them and that I wasn't a wimp. So he sent me a list of obscenities which I duly reamed off at them all one night. I roared these swear words like a trooper. Things improved after that and they became friendly. I was able to get them on my side then. In fact it worked so well that I was elected as group leader. I was really delighted because it had been a difficult few weeks.' Valerie's use of 'obscene language' as a rite of passage into the group might sound wooden or hollow in the 1990s, but it was probably a stroke of genius at a time when a 'Lady' simply didn't use the language of the street. But Valerie always has a way of transcending her own level. She has the common touch.

'Once I got them on my side we were able to get things done. One thing that needed doing was washing. Some of the girls would not wash. Perhaps they came from very deprived backgrounds but there were some with head lice and all sorts of things. One girl I remember in particular. We had to clip the clothes from her body. They were stuck to her with dirt. She really stank. The whole group told her that we had to do it. It wasn't just me. We cut them off of her and then gave her a shower. She did shower after that and she was more comfortable. Now, the head lice business wasn't very pleasant but it had to be done.' Valerie's ability to muck in must have impressed her commanding officers, as no doubt did the fact that she was chosen as the group's leader despite their initial reservations about her accent and title.

Following basic training, Valerie spent a short period as 'glorified clerk'. 'It wasn't even that glorified actually. I was filling in forms for guns and things. I was hopeless. I'm very bad at doing repetitive jobs and I made terrible mistakes. But I was moved and luckily I was sent to cadet-training school in Leicestershire. I think that lasted about three months. There were about six hundred of us there. That training was more geared towards leadership. I remember writing essays about the kind of people I would try and save if Britain's leaders and important people were involved in a crash. The idea was to explain the sort of people who could rebuild Britain after the war. At the end of the officer training I came out first of the group. I was pleased about that. The passing out was a great day and all the girls' parents were invited. I don't think they understood the concept of husbands. I remember that Basil came but he wasn't quite sure how to conduct himself in front of the head ATS. He wasn't sure whether to salute them or not.'

Having passed out with flying colours, Valerie was sent to Windsor where the Grenadier Guards were then based. As a second lieutenant she became a platoon commander with a hundred or so women in her charge. In Windsor, the women's job was to look after the secretarial and cooking duties for the anti-aircraft unit stationed there, though women often operated the searchlights. Valerie was pleased to be stationed near London because amongst other things it meant she was near her mother. But being almost permanently stationed also meant that she could set about establishing a proper home for Nanny, young Lingard and herself and Basil. In 1943 they found 'a lovely little house in Egham which is very near to Windsor. We weren't there long when the doodlebugs started, but again we were lucky and none fell near us. Once when I was travelling between Windsor and Egham I heard one coming and I threw myself off my motorbike. At the time I was frightened that I might be expecting, because I had just had the German measles, and between the fright and the fall I had a miscarriage. It sounds awful to say it but it was probably just as well.'

Egham was a typical London suburb: it was leafy and quiet and had a common. At the edge of the common stands a pub called The Barley Mow, which in those days was run by a 'lovely man called Dick'. 'We would drink there every Sunday when we were on leave. We often drank during the blackout, beer mostly because drink was hard to come by. I remember thinking Dick had great courage because some white American soldiers refused to drink in the same room as their black colleagues. Colour was a big problem then, but Dick wouldn't have any of it. If the white boys wouldn't drink with the blacks then they could leave as far as he was concerned. Dick worked very hard. It wasn't easy running a pub during the war. Once when he got away for a break I ran the pub for him.'

Valerie was a bit disappointed to find that The Barley Mow had been fitted out with jukeboxes when she returned there in 1993. Otherwise little had changed. The back garden was fitted out with tables and chairs, and people still took their pints of ale onto the common, though it was forbidden. The stay in Egham was a happy time for Valerie. She and Basil were often able to organise their leave together, and with Windsor only a couple of miles away, Valerie was able to spend a lot of time at home with Nanny and Lingard.

By 1944, Valerie was keen to have another baby. Although Basil wasn't a child enthusiast, he accepted Valerie's point that it was better for her to have children when they weren't able to do anything exciting with their lives. 'I was allowed to stay in the army until about three or four months into the pregnancy. I had a chance of going to staff college, but Basil wanted our children to be born in Ireland, regardless of the fact that I would be alone in Ireland. I didn't like the idea of going back because I only knew people there because of Basil. The lease was up on Castleknock, so my mother organised a cottage for me in Palmerstown. I went back to Ireland on a plane from Speke airport in Liverpool. I remember that I got stuck in the loo on the plane because I was so big, and they had to take the door off to get me out. Can you imagine? Of course with the war there were very few friends about, but some older people helped me out. I just remember being very lonely and feeling on my own. I was induced in the end and it was an easier birth than Lingard had been, but that was because Tim was smaller. He was about eight and a half pounds. I had gas and some injections which made the whole thing much better. I was just furious being in Ireland and missing the end of the war in Europe. VE Day was 8 May and there I was alone. I wrote to Basil and told him to enjoy it and he wrote back telling me how great it had been. I was mad. Getting the news of the baby to Basil wasn't easy, but the air attaché here in Dublin was very helpful. You see you couldn't just send telegrams as you wanted. So I remember he sent off a wire to Basil saying that "another Mustang has arrived safely". That was how Basil knew it was a boy.'

Valerie's cousin, Sir James Colyer-Fergusson, got out of a prisoner-of-war camp not long after Tim was born. Polly was very worried about him because she knew that he had had a rough time in camps in Germany and Poland. James didn't talk about the experience much, but Valerie did find out that he had been chained to a wall for six months during his incarceration. Polly sent him to Valerie in Ireland, hoping that she could begin his recuperation with the slightly better rations that were available here. 'I tried to get James to eat up, but he couldn't manage a lot because of the condition he was in. I was determined to get back to Egham as soon as I could, and that meant bringing a small baby over by boat. Poor James wasn't that used to babies and I remember that we nearly left poor Tim on the Holyhead train. I thought it would be good to get James to enjoy himself, so I took him to a night spot when we got to London, but he was so exhausted he just slept. I was only back in Egham a few weeks when Margaret Biddle rang me up and told me she was having trouble with the American Services Club in London. She wanted me to come and help. Margaret was the wife of Anthony Drexel-Biddle who was American ambassador to the occupied countries. He had been in Poland but had managed to get out. I liked both of them very much. After talking to Margaret, I ended up running the club, which was very interesting because you met all sorts of people. The Americans had food, unlike the rest of England, so their men would use the club to meet and have meals and relax. I organised the use of the rooms, who could stay, and made the food arrangements.'

Valerie liked Americans, and particularly enjoyed meeting war correspondents at the dinners she attended at the American embassy. 'Ed Murrow was a great commentator. His broadcasts were often on the BBC. I really liked him, and another was Ned Russell. His wife Mary was in the American Red Cross. We became great friends. They weren't like Mrs Simpson, they knew about England and its history.' Though life was by no means easy in London in the months following the end of the war in Europe, Valerie remembers it as a good time. She was meeting interesting people, including Lord and Lady Mountbatten, and she had 'something to do' with her work for the Americans. The war had been good to Valerie. Unlike many women who were parted from their husbands for the whole war, she had rarely been away from Basil for longer than six months, and they had always managed to get leave together so that they could meet up.

Ironically, while the war kept Basil and Valerie together, a sporting injury kept them apart for quite some time during 1946 and 1947. 'Basil had a bad back injury as a result of a kick while playing football. During the war it got worse and he had to wear a steel brace. Eventually, after the war, it got so bad that he was flat on his back most of the time. In the end he arranged for a top RAF surgeon to operate on him. It was an awful operation and involved the grafting of some bone from his hip onto his spine. The recuperation took a long time and he spent ages in hospital in London, and then ages with his mother in the country. My mother looked after him as well. He spent a long time on his back. It was very grim. In fact he knew that he was going to be out for a while so we both thought it was a good time to have another baby while he could do nothing.' One of the positive aspects of Basil's long recovery was that he developed his life-long passion for gardening. Valerie cannot now remember whether it was her mother or Basil's who gave him some gardening books, but once he got interested he was hooked for life. From the moment that he bought Dargle Cottage the development of its garden was to be a consuming interest. Luckily, Basil had organised the purchase of Dargle, before going into hospital, so although Valerie had to do a lot of travelling in order to see him, she at least had a home of her own to do it from.

This must have been a demanding period for Valerie who had two small children and one on the way. Basil's letters are full of instructions in relation to the restoration of Dargle and the organisation of men to carry out all sorts of work. One senses that much of her energy at this time must have been taken up with activity that by nature would not have greatly interested her, as many people would point out that 'Lady G wouldn't notice if the piano was carried out of the livingroom in front of her eyes'. From their correspondence it is clear that absence was making the heart grow fonder. Reading their letters, one cannot but be conscious of the consuming and exclusive passion they felt for each other. So if Valerie found herself involved in tasks that she would not normally have enjoyed, they were carried out as a labour of love:

Darlingest,

You have been looking so lovely lately that I want you to be colour photographed by the greatest expert. You should be in your blue evening dress with Victorian necklace of gold and bracelet ditto, hand raised to show its grace . . . .

Thank you most truly, my darling, for trailing along to see me every day wet or fine. It makes the world of difference even when I felt too congested to talk. Must say I doubt if I'd have come in here if I'd known the horror of the first week.[3]

Basil spent the Christmas of 1946 flat on his back at his mother's house, Ropley:

Pretty exhaustive experiments here seem to say that alcohol, in small doses anyhow, don't make no difference; so I'm putting myself on a slight lunch-hour binge of white wine. The ruddy itch hangs on, but is not so fierce as formerly, and carbolic daubing helps it. Only a week or so to 'half-term' . . . .

Spent a lot of time around Xmas wondering what you were all up to. Me Oh My, I do look forward to a little Honey with you when you're a willowy pink Dianthus again and I a wickedly active Seducer. Meantime I keep body and soul together by nice thinks about you and lots of fussings that you're being a good strong careful Stork.[4]

In retrospect, the period between Valerie's marriage and the beginnings of her involvement in the establishment of the Central Remedial Clinic can almost be viewed as a time of preparation: preparation for a period when she would be able to 'do something' with her life. Listening to her talk about the war years, one realises that her main priority was to stay as close as she could to Basil. Their love affair was her consuming interest. She saw the war as having robbed them of much of the fun she might have expected as a newly-wed. Valerie wanted to use that wasted time to have a family so that when it was over she could get on with living. In the immediate aftermath of the war her life was dominated by travelling to and from Basil's sick-bed, by house repairs and renovations, and by pregnancy. But only a part of her was satisfied. As the 1940s drew to a close Valerie Goulding searched for something to do.

---

1 *English History 1914–1945*. A J P Taylor. Oxford University Press, Oxford 1992, p499.
2 Basil's RAF documents in Lady Goulding's possession.
3 Basil to Valerie from London, 21 November 1946.
4 *Ibid*. 31 December 1946.

5

THE CENTRAL REMEDIAL CLINIC

Hers is an extraordinary achievement. I hope she feels that her life's work was worth it all and that she enjoyed what she was doing: and not for *noblesse oblige* or to be seen to be doing it or to play to the gallery. I hope that she got great pleasure out of doing it in her own life. I really hope she did because she sacrificed everything else for it.

Ken Holden's assessment of Valerie's commitment to her work for the Central Remedial Clinic highlights a view of her that dominates the thinking of many people who have been close to the CRC since it was founded. It is hard to find anyone who will question the single-mindedness of her dedication, but many will query whether the price of her commitment was the forfeiture of the rest of her life.

Valerie always wanted to be a doctor. 'As a child I was very interested in medicine and I was good at first aid. I remember that when I was about twelve the chauffeur's mother fell and broke her leg and there was no doctor available. I made up a pair of splints and strapped them to her leg. The chauffeur was pleased because he was worried about his mother, but when she got to the hospital the doctor wanted to know who or what had applied the splints! Another time when we were out driving, my mother ran over a bird. I said that we couldn't leave it half alive and begged her to stop the car. She was horrified and asked me if I was proposing to wring its neck. I would have tried if it were necessary. Thank goodness it was already dead. As I grew up I always said that I wanted to be a doctor; the truth is I probably wouldn't have had the academic ability. But it was something I thought about a lot. After the war and after I had had three children I suppose I thought it

86

was too late to start a seven-year medical course. I didn't have the qualifications anyway and I realised that if I attempted it I would never be at home.'

Coming back to Ireland after the war, Valerie found herself very conscious of poverty. 'The poverty didn't seem so bad in England. Everyone seemed to have a ration book. Even on St Stephen's Green there were children without shoes. I began working in Marrowbone Lane a couple of days a week. It was a sort of soup kitchen where poor people got a meal. I used to do the wash-up. There was one boy in particular. He was so thin. He used to get a pill and a meal. It was awful. I had a natural reaction to poverty and I knew that I had to do more than just wash up.'

In the late 1940s Valerie met the woman who would shine the torch and point her in the direction that would absorb her for the rest of her life. Kathleen O'Rourke was a remedial gymnast with a special interest in rehabilitation therapy. She ran the Irish branch of the League of Health and Beauty and was responsible for setting up the first antenatal classes for women in Dublin. One woman who remembers Valerie and Kathleen from the early days of their association is Joan Carr, a physiotherapist who was unlucky enough to contract polio in the 1960s. 'My mother used to go along to Kathleen's health and gymnastic classes in Bewley's restaurant in Grafton Street. They were very popular amongst young and middle-aged housewives. Kathleen was very slim and fit and used to wear black satin panties and a white satin sleeveless top when she was performing the exercises. I'll always remember her with her leg cocked up high on the counter showing the women how to do the various positions. She was well versed in anatomy and knew about muscle development, relaxation and breathing. She was an early pioneer of prenatal classes in Ireland, and that's where she applied her knowledge of breathing and relaxation techniques so well. I knew her until she died, but it was when I contracted polio myself and went to the Central Remedial Clinic for help that I saw her very regularly. She was a lovely person.'

Like many successful combinations, one cannot imagine two more unlikely partners than Valerie and Kathleen. By all accounts Kathleen was a quiet and modest person. She was single, and was related to the archbishop of Dublin, John Charles McQuaid. What drew the two women together was a desire to do something about the lack of after-care facilities for polio victims in Dublin in the late 1940s. Kathleen had the local knowledge and the rehabilitation skills: Valerie had the organisational talent, the social contacts and a burning desire to be active. Máirín Byrne, who has been responsible for the development of the school facilities at the CRC, feels that Kathleen and Valerie had one very significant quality in common: both were looking for a niche in life. 'Kathleen was a slightly Anglo-Irish person and she was somewhat marginalised by the new breed of trained physiotherapists. She had a quasi-medical background. She was a woman looking for a cause.' Valerie regarded Kathleen as a 'serious person. Like many people that I knew, the war had robbed her of happiness. She had been engaged to an RAF flyer, a Scotsman, but he was killed. He was on his way back from Germany and lost control of his plane. He crashed and lost both legs. He died later. She used to speak about him quite a bit. She had a lot of friends in England. She was very Irish and Catholic, but she wasn't anti-Protestant.

'It was Kathleen who suggested that I should study physiotherapy if I couldn't manage a seven-year course to be a doctor. I thought it was a great idea so in 1949 I enrolled in the Dublin School of Physiotherapy in Hume Street.' Joan Carr was in Valerie's class. 'I remember the first day of term, we were just a bunch of schoolgirls and then this woman walked in who was much older than the rest of us. Miss Allen introduced her and said that she was Mrs Goulding. As the days went by it became clear that she had three children, which all seemed very strange. We thought that she was a poor widow because her husband was never in evidence. You never heard about him – just the boys. Some of us thought that she was getting a profession so that she could bring the boys up. Then it leaked that she was Lady Goulding and this caused a bit of excitement. She had been trying to be discreet. I think she parked her car, a lovely silver Healy sports, around the corner at first so as not to attract attention. She was very attractive: tall, thin and athletic. It wasn't that she paid a great deal of attention to what she wore but she was very attractive to look at. There were no airs and graces or the latest fashion, but she was very likeable. Once we knew who she was, she used to pile us all into her car and take us to play squash in Fitzwilliam, which was in Lad Lane in those days. There's one funny thing I remember about her. For our classes we wore white coats, but when we were doing our gymnastics we would change into a brown gym frock and brown knickers. When the time came to do somersaults we'd tuck our frocks into our knickers. But you can imagine what Lady G looked like with her long legs. She looked really funny and gawky, but she always had her homework done.

'It was only afterwards I realised how difficult it must have been for her because she often went to England at the weekends to see Lingard. I think it was one of the reasons that she gave up in the end. She was a perfectionist and she had a lot of other commitments which made it difficult for her to get the study done. I suppose another factor was that the need for some kind of after-care service was growing. There was a polio epidemic in 1948 and in early 1950, and the victims were piling up. In those days you had Cork Street Hospital and that was it really. The Cork Street physios hadn't the time for much after-care. People had no place to go, and if they could get treatment how could they get there? It was vital that something was set up because without treatment the muscles of polio victims just atrophied.'

A number of factors combined to force Valerie to leave the Dublin School of Physiotherapy. 'It was a three-year course and I was finding it hard to keep up. I was working at night so that I wouldn't fall behind. Then I had a miscarriage which meant that I was out for a while. But more importantly, the more I saw of the polio situation, the more I realised that after-care and helping mothers get their children to and from a treatment centre was the real problem. There was only one physiotherapist per hospital at the time, and no occupational therapy. When we visited hospitals and saw the children it was obvious that something had to be done. I discussed it with Kathleen. I asked her if she thought it would be better for me to leave the course after two of the three years and start a small centre for polio rehabilitation. In the end we agreed to start something but I was determined to find out as much as I could about modern treatment and what was possible, before we tried to help. I wanted to do things properly.'

A most important factor in the initial success and later development of the CRC was that Valerie's approach was businesslike. Nowadays, many of her critics might question the clinic's apparent focus on one person's contribution, or query her hands-on methods, but even a cursory study of the way she set about establishing the clinic shows that she was no 'do-gooder'. While it would be going too far to suggest that she had an overall strategy in those early days, she was definitely determined to provide the most up-to-date treatments available, with the help of people who understood the latest trends in rehabilitation treatment. Geraldine Cruess-Callaghan was on the first CRC organising committee and remained a governor until the late 1980s. She points out that the essence of Valerie's strength was that 'unlike me, Valerie did not have an emotional reaction to seeing these little children with contorted limbs. She never let her heart rule her head. She knew there was something to be done and that she had to do it'.

Both Kathleen and Valerie were aware that they could do nothing without the help and cooperation of the medical establishment, so they sought a meeting with Doctor J Boyd Dunlop, a young consultant orthopaedic surgeon based in Dublin's Fitzwilliam Place. He recalled his first meeting with them. 'It was some time at the end of 1950 or the beginning of 1951 when they came to these consulting rooms here. In fact I can see the two of them sitting in front of me as if it were yesterday. We talked about the polio epidemic and the problems associated with the care of these children when they returned to their families. We agreed that the after-care being provided was not what it should have been. The tendency at the time was for orthopaedic surgeons to put the children into hospital and keep them there for treatment. That meant that they were frequently in hospital for long periods of time with varying amounts of physiotherapy. In many cases the children were in hospital in the first place because their homes were poor and they were getting poor home care – not of course through any fault of their parents. Kathleen and Valerie felt very strongly about the provision of better after-care, and what they wanted was my opinion about how to go about improving it.

'We found that our ideas were the same. They wanted to keep the children out of hospital and I agreed. From the beginning, the basic aim of the clinic was to avoid hospital treatment. We all met at just the right moment and I think that the meeting benefited everyone. I was ready to be developed, and it was the right time for me to get involved in this new way of treating polio patients. I was already a regular visitor to many foreign clinics and I was trying to broaden my experience and knowledge, and to understand new methods. I had just been appointed a consultant at Dr Steeven's Hospital, and I was also at the hospital in Clontarf. I was responsible for assessing war injuries for the British Department of Health in Dublin, and as a result I was conscious of what could be done even in the most horrendous of circumstances.'

Valerie always emphasises the fact that the Dublin Remedial Clinic, as it was first called, was started on a shoestring. She never fails to tell interviewers that Kathleen and herself had only a few pounds in their purses when they started making plans for the clinic. In playing up its humble beginnings and highlighting its association with the fund-raising efforts of Queenie, the doyenne of the traders on Dublin's Moore Street, and the men at the Hanlon's Corner cattle market, Valerie ensures that the legend of the CRC's plebeian beginnings is maintained. The reality is somewhat different. Whether or not Valerie had five or a hundred pounds in her purse in 1951 is irrelevant: what mattered was that she knew a lot of people who did have money in their pockets, and more importantly she was able to gather around the new venture the kind of people who would make it successful.

One of the first people that Valerie successfully inveigled into supporting the clinic was Geraldine Cruess-Callaghan, who had first met the Gouldings when they moved to Shankill on the south side of Dublin. Geraldine and her husband Cedric were regular attenders at the Saturday night dinner dance at Kilcroney Golf Club. 'Even then Valerie would be talking to someone in the corner, telling them all about the need for after-care. No matter where she was, no matter what party, Valerie would be trying to win support for her project. My husband Cedric was very fond of her and he said he'd help, but when it came to the actual start-up of the clinic, she went into Cedric's offices in town and of course he sent her out to me. So that was the beginning of my involvement. The first time I worked with Valerie, she told me to bring my car as we were going to collect some children who needed physiotherapy and bring them to Kathleen's flat. It all started in that small flat of Kathleen's on Upper Pembroke Street. We used to have to carry the children up three flights of stairs to her sittingroom. I always remember one small boy that Valerie normally collected from Oliver Bond flats. She'd drive the car right into the complex so that it would be easy to get the child into the car. Needless to say the spectacle of Valerie and her car was quite an occasion, with all the women and the children hanging out over the balconies. The little fella that she was collecting looked Valerie straight in the eye and said to her "Are you a Protestant Mrs?". "Why do you ask?" said Valerie. "Because me mammy says you're the spitting image of one." ' By June 1951 news of Valerie's and Kathleen's efforts were beginning to get attention in the newspapers:

> Lady Goulding, the organising director, has been thinking about the matter for a couple of years, and plans are now in line for the foundation of the clinic. All that remains to be achieved is the collection of £20,000.
>
> It is going to be a big effort, but supporters of the scheme are optimistic, and hope to raise sufficient money by the end of the year. All subscriptions will be accounted for by trustees, among whom are two governors of the Bank of Ireland, and Miss Eva Murphy, whose interest in health matters in this city is well known. Among the societies with which she is associated are the Women's National Health Association and the Peamount After-Care Guild.
>
> The Dublin Remedial Clinic will not overlap any existing hospital service – in fact, it will considerably help the hospital authorities. Poliomyelitis treatment is divided into three stages – hospitalisation, post hospital treatment and rehabilitation.
>
> The International Infantile Paralysis Fellowship, which does such valuable work for those in the last-mentioned stage, is now at work here, and an Irish branch was formed in Dublin some years ago. This body is working in close cooperation with the organisers of the Dublin Remedial Clinic, who will pass on their patients to the Fellowship when the time comes, so that they may be re-absorbed into normal or near-normal life.
>
> Although the clinic is not built, the work has already started . . . . At the moment the patients, many of them completely immobile, are carried up three flights of stairs for their daily treatment of specially graded exercises to limber up paralysed muscles. The latest methods of treatment are used. These will be continued and augmented in the clinic, which will also treat asthma and postural defects, with the sanction of the medical profession and the Department of Health.[1]

Doctor Dunlop remembers that the first children were treated on the table in Kathleen's sittingroom. 'In the beginning Kathleen did the driving as well, but as the volume increased, Valerie took that over and organised a team of voluntary drivers so that Kathleen could get on with the physiotherapy. The fact that we very quickly got a band of drivers meant that the numbers being brought increased. The children were always referred by doctors, but I saw them and made my own assessment. Then Kathleen would put into effect the programme that had been agreed in each case.' Children from all over the city were ferried by Valerie and her crew of middle-class ladies. In general though, the children came from poor families where mothers were hard put to get a child with polio to and from hospital.

At the outset, Valerie was largely occupied during daylight hours with driving, but her real preoccupation was how to fund the proposed new clinic. She told the inaugural meeting of the clinic's trustees on 1 May 1951 that five hundred pounds had been collected and she suggested that a small central committee of four be formed to arrange the fundraising. Apart from Valerie there was Nora Fitzgerald, the wine merchant, Geraldine Cruess-Callaghan and William Martin Murphy:

> It was stated by Lady Goulding that several social activities had been arranged to aid the campaign for raising funds, including a polo match during Horse Show week, a small scale car rally organised by Mr Mc Carthy Filgate and that a day's takings had been offered by the proprietors of the following houses: Russell Hotel, Bailey Restaurant, Hibernian Buttery, Dolphin Hotel, Shelbourne Rooms and Redbank Restaurant. Mr Browne suggested that solicitors be consulted on the advisability of running a sweepstakes or pool on jockeys.[2]

As the list of hostelries above shows, the committee's social connections ensured from the start that the clinic would receive wide and generous support. The minutes of the second meeting on 22 May record: 'The idea of a mile of sixpences was discussed by the Committee and Mr Murphy agreed to ask the Lord Mayor for permission to use the pavements on Stephen's Green. Miss Fitzgerald suggested approaching the race horse owners and the Turf Club for permission to run a Nomination Race . . . . Also it might be possible to get a gift of a yearling to sell in the August Sales.'[3]

Valerie's committee hardly lacked for fundraising ideas, and from the beginning they planned their money-making activities around both large and small events:

> Lady Goulding, organising director of the recently formed Dublin Remedial Clinic, left Dublin last week in the *Irish Pine* for the United States. By now she should have arrived, and be in the first stopping-place of her American tour – Washington. She has gone to America to interest the people there in the Dublin Remedial Clinic, and to ask for dollars for its upkeep and expansion.
>
> Her visit will take about a month, and during that time she will visit New York, Philadelphia and Boston. Fortified by the knowledge that she has many friends in America and that infantile paralysis is a matter of public concern there, Lady Goulding should not have much trouble in achieving her object, for the Clinic has been established for the post-hospital treatment of this disease.
>
> Boston on St Patrick's Day is usually given over to the Irish. This year, there will be something extra, for a special reception is being given for Lady Goulding by the medical profession. By that time she will have been joined by yet another director of the Clinic, Mrs Geraldine Callaghan, who is leaving for the United States this week.
>
> While she is in the USA Lady Goulding will offer for sale, a family document which has been handed down to her great-grandfather, who was a physician to Queen Victoria. It is a prescription written by him for the Queen.[4]

Valerie had two purposes in mind when she sailed to America aboard a great old cargo boat, the *Irish Pine*, at the beginning of March 1952. She had high hopes of significant fundraising, and she was anxious to see as much as she could of the latest American rehabilitation practices. She speaks with great affection about the *Pine* and remembers the journey over as a great adventure. 'I really did want to do everything properly, and I asked many people in Dublin who was the best person in the rehabilitation area. Many doctors, including Dr Dunlop, suggested that I see Dr Howard Rusk in New York. I had to ask Basil for the money, but I was determined to go and see him and find out as much as I could. There was only one other passenger on the *Irish Pine*. He was on his way to America to get a job in a garage. Captain Kelly was terrific because it wasn't the best of crossings. We had terrible weather. We had to heave to for a couple of days, and we ended up landing in St John's in Canada. But we kept our spirits up, playing cards with the engineer and the first officer.'

Geraldine Cruess-Callaghan travelled out a week or so later to meet Valerie and remembers the visit as one long tour of the hospitals in New York and Boston, with Valerie keenly absorbing everything she could learn. Dr Rusk was professor and chairman at the Department of Rehabilitation Medicine, New York University Medical Centre, and was internationally renowned for his pioneering work with disabled people. Valerie was conscious of needing to overcome the image of the madwoman trying to do good, and was determined to get Dr Rusk's help. 'When I met him he asked me if I really was going to do something. He was a great big kind man and I think he looked at me with a certain surprise. He asked me a lot of questions about what I was trying to do and who was involved in Ireland. The good thing was that once he'd checked me out he let me into the hospital several days running. I suppose the main difference about the way he thought about rehabilitation then was that he asked a person to try and be mobile even if it hurt. He had a lot of polio victims there, so I was able to see what way he was handling the treatment. He also suggested that I go up to the Boston Children's Hospital, which I did. I will never forget the young doctor that I met there. He was probably only thirty or so, but he had contracted polio during his work with the children. He was badly affected. He was terribly gnarled and just looked so sad. That remained with me – it seemed so hard. Dr Rusk really did convince me of the need for physiotherapy. Some doctors in Ireland who hadn't seen the effects of physiotherapy on war injuries, simply didn't realise how much it could change the quality of life of a person with polio. After talking with Dr Rusk I was much better able to talk to doctors at home.'

While Valerie benefited significantly from a medical perspective on her first trip to America, she was a little disappointed with the scale of the fundraising. Geraldine Cruess-Callaghan feels that 'the first few trips were not so well organised. Sometimes the people who were meant to be arranging events were enthralled by the prospect of meeting a "Lady". Because of that, I don't think the first few American visits were very successful'. Valerie's letters to Basil while she was in

America show how concerned she was about the effectiveness of some of the people who had promised support. From Boston she wrote:

> Darling this is awful. I don't see a prospect of raising a cent. The UDHs arrived Wednesday night and kept talking of the hard work they had done but so far all I can see is that I am meeting their friends on the 17th who are neither rich or willing to fork out. They never stop talking from 9 am until midnight and get nothing done. I am just trying to plough ahead on my own with the introductions I have, and hope to do something but feel rather pessimistic . . . .
>
> Oh Darling I do wish you were here I miss you so very much, I am longing to come home . . . . Your very pessimistic and disillusioned Pie.[5]

From Washington she wrote:

> Darlingest, I love you so very much and miss you more each day. I really do, and don't know how I am going to be able to stay over here; but I feel I must, just to see if I can do anything for the clinic. We have definitely been had for mugs in Boston, and I think all the UDHs were doing were bringing out their daughter on the title.[6]

Valerie would have had no objection at all to her title being used to ease some young lady's entrance into the Boston social scene, had the clinic benefited by a significant donation: apparently it did not. But things began to look up near the end of March when Valerie rang Colonel Berk, a friend of her father's, who was the vice-president of an advertising firm, Warwick and Legler. In a letter to Basil she wrote that the colonel had been 'wonderful' and had taken complete charge of their campaign in the United States. 'We really feel quite encouraged at last. But a big but – we shall have to return in October all expenses paid and make a tour rather like Princess Elizabeth, and we should raise well over three hundred thousand dollars, anyhow I will discuss it all on return. I can't tell you how I am longing to get home.'[7] On her return, Valerie told a trustees meeting that she had collected about two thousand dollars in America, in small subscriptions. She explained that they would not be able to receive large contributions until the clinic was registered as a company in America, whereupon the donors would be able to claim a rebate off their income tax. Her message to the trustees was upbeat. She told them that Colonel Berk had placed the fundraising for the clinic in the hands of a Mr Lee who anticipated being able to raise between two hundred and three hundred thousand dollars. She also told the meeting that it was her understanding that the fundraising services would be paid for by Warwick and Legler.

In July, David Lee travelled to Ireland to meet the clinic's directors. According to the minutes Mr Lee told them that:

> when Lady Goulding and Mrs Callaghan were in the States and had talked about a campaign for raising money for the clinic, the feasible amount estimated then was 300,000$. Since then, Mr Lee had been speaking to people who were close to fund-raising activities in the States, and he now thought that 100,000$ would be nearer the mark. He said that he would aim at 300,000$ and then if we got 100,000$ it would be a job well done. Mr Lee said that he estimated the time needed to raise such a sum at five to six months. The actual time that the directors should be in the States would be about six weeks. He recommended that the whole tour should be arranged professionally and that an American Council should be set up as soon as possible.[8]

David Lee recommended the setting up of as many local committees in America as possible. He also suggested that rural areas would make good locations for the committees, as they would be likely to have a lot of Irish priests who would be willing to help promote the clinic. He stressed the importance of having the support of both the Irish and American Roman Catholic hierarchies for any proposed tour of the States, and particularly advised that the backing of Dr McQuaid, the archbishop of Dublin, was essential. David Lee estimated that it would cost the clinic about ten thousand dollars in agents' fees alone to arrange the proposed American tour, and confirmed that while his company, Ray McCarthy, did not like short-term contracts, they would handle the trip on a once-off basis.

Reading both the minutes and Valerie's letters in 1951 and 1952, one is struck by her enthusiasm and commitment to getting the clinic off the ground. There was, however, also a sense of her over-optimistic expectation of the outcome of her various efforts. She was endowed with the very Irish trait of expecting that mountains could be moved because someone somewhere knew her father or had made the family's acquaintance. This is abundantly clear from her newly formed committee's cautious reaction to her first trip to the United States. After her report on the potential earnings that could accrue from the involvement of the Ray McCarthy Organisation, and the promise that 'on account of Lady Goulding's personal contact' the clinic would not be charged for the American firm's services, the committee unanimously agreed that it would be a good idea to get the whole thing in writing. Typically, Valerie was happy with her verbal understanding with her father's friend Colonel Berk. The minutes show that Valerie's trust and optimism were, on this occasion, misplaced:

> The content of a letter dated 17 October 1952 from Mr David Lee of the Ray McCarthy Organisation were fully discussed. His report on work done on behalf of the Clinic was considered very unsatisfactory and the question of paying his account of $1,313.54 arose. It was decided that:
>
> 1. Miss Nora Fitzgerald should write to Mr John Leslie, USA (a member of the Council of the Friends of Central Remedial Clinic of Ireland) requesting advice with regard to the future dealings of the Clinic with the Ray McCarthy Organisation.
> 2. That Mr Browne should write a personal letter to Mr Kennedy informing him of the present position between the Clinic and the Ray McCarthy Organisation and asking him for any suggestions.
> 3. That, subject to the approval of Mr Nolan, Solicitor, Lady Goulding should write to Mr Lee to the effect that the Directors and Trustees were very disappointed in the results of the Ray McCarthy Organisation's efforts to raise funds for the Clinic, which was carrying on with great difficulty, and stating that his account would have to receive their very careful consideration.[9]

Although Valerie's enthusiasm and optimism might have been occasionally off the mark, there is no doubt that these same qualities injected the breath of life necessary to get the clinic off the ground. In the months after the clinic took its first patients, the minutes highlight the essential Valerie Goulding: reading them, one can almost see her bounding into meetings suggesting schemes, thinking up ways of getting around difficulties, and all the time attempting to convince people that what she wanted could be done. From the beginning she insisted on the need to publicise the clinic's work, regarding a high profile as the key to fundraising. Often the committee or the trustees advised that she hold off on ventures, including a plan to make a film about the clinic, on the basis that it was ill-advised, given the clinic's available funds. From Valerie's point of view such caution was a mistake. She approached the whole problem of polio and disability from the perspective of a marketing executive, and that meant identifying the cause, highlighting the need and then appealing for a public response. Unlike charities that were previously organised in Ireland, Valerie's idea was to operate in a very high-profile way. The result of that policy would later transform disability and its treatment into an almost glamorous cause, so effective was she in establishing the clinic's fundraising image on Ireland's social scene.

However, long before Valerie became a celebrity, she was displaying a great ability to enthuse strangers about her cause. Geraldine Cruess-Callaghan, herself no mean achiever when it came to organising money-making ventures, remembers the night when, in a stroke, Valerie secured the CRC's first proper premises. 'We had been operating out of Kathleen's flat on Pembroke Street for about two years at that stage, and we were very anxious to move to somewhere more suitable. It was becoming more and more difficult to run the clinic, even though we had taken additional space on the ground floor of the Pembroke house. Things were better than they had been at first. We had more drivers, which meant more patients, and we were getting to the stage where we needed a secretary and additional physiotherapists. But space and staff were a problem. Then one night in the spring of 1953, Basil, Valerie, my husband Cedric and I were having dinner in Jammet's restaurant. As usual, Valerie was talking about the clinic. We were sitting in the front room of the restaurant which wasn't very big. Unknown to us, the couple at the other table had been listening to our conversation and near the end of the meal a man came over from the other table and introduced himself. He said that he had been listening for a half an hour or so and was very impressed with all he had heard. He said that it all sounded very remarkable. His name was Major Beaumont,[10] and once we asked him and his wife to join us, Valerie was off. She told him about how the clinic was being run from a room with the help of a lot of volunteers and she explained that we really needed a new premises. He asked a number of questions, and there and then offered to double whatever we were able to raise. Needless to say he became our next governor, and within a year we moved to Goatstown. It was a pity that he didn't live to see the clinic make the big move to Clontarf. But it was amazing that so much came out of that chance meeting. Perhaps his generosity had something to do with the fact that he didn't have any children.'

In many respects the Major Beaumont story epitomises Valerie's great ability in the early days of the clinic to gather willing helpers around her. As Doctor Boyd Dunlop emphasises, 'no one person could do everything, but she got a band of very good people together. It didn't matter whether those people worked in the kitchen or in the physiotherapy department, or whether they were on the medical side, she was able to imbue people with enthusiasm. People worked hard for the clinic and I think that she always got on well with them.' Geraldine Cruess-Callaghan acknowledges the input of the many people who contributed their time and money in the early 1950s. But casting a cold, dispassionate eye, she holds that it was Valerie's determination to succeed and the fact that she was a titled lady, that combined to make the clinic a success. 'She was a woman seeking a mission. She didn't have time for anything else. She was kindness itself but she was single-minded about it. It simply would not have got off the ground without her. She never talked about anything else. Often if you hadn't seen her for a while, she'd say come down and let's have a talk. But when you'd get there it would always be the clinic. And of course the title was very important. People always wanted to meet Lady Goulding both here and in America. And she didn't mind using it if it helped raise money.'

Another of the clinic's governors, Noel Judd, also acknowledges the importance of Valerie's title. 'The title is a very special thing; it has pulling power. People were very happy to be associated with the clinic, and one big factor was her name and title. She had a great ability to meet the right people and persuade them to support our efforts. I had got involved in the first place through my wife Georgie. She became one of the early volunteer drivers, and through her I met Valerie, who asked me to become a governor. I arranged the purchase of Prospect Hall in Goatstown in 1954 and organised the building and refurbishment programme. Georgie became very involved in the fundraising and ended up running two dances a year, including the big New Year's Eve ball. That was always splendidly patronised. Ken Besson used to give us the ballroom in the Hibernian Hotel for nothing in those days. But we got great pleasure out of it being part of the clinic. My wife loved children; we had a big family ourselves and I remember Georgie's delight when she saw a boy that she had collected and carried up the three flights of stairs in Pembroke Street as a toddler, playing football many years later as a young teenager.'

Looking through the minutes of the various clinic committees in the early days, it is obvious that while the demand for the CRC's services was growing, frustration often arose out of the voluntary nature of the help available. With children being ferried from all over the city, the organisation of a drivers' roster was of vital importance to the smooth running of the operation. Geraldine Cruess-Callaghan is noted in an August 1953 minute as describing the drivers' system as chaotic. 'It was agreed that this matter should be left for Mrs Callaghan to deal with.' Apart from the acquisition of a proper premises, the trustees and fundraisers also faced the problem of providing enough general staff and physiotherapists to meet the workload. Although there were many drawbacks in the way the clinic was initially organised, the voluntary and communal effort involved would remain its distinguishing hallmark. When the State took over the main funding, many of the old hands feared that the essential voluntary spirit would be lost. So while Valerie perhaps exaggerates a little the role played by Queenie in Moore Street, or Basil's efforts with the collector's box, in the actual generation of funds she is genuinely reflecting the essence of how the CRC was developed through the unpaid efforts of all kinds of people who responded to her call for help.

By 1954 that call for help was beginning to show results. The clinic's new premises at Prospect Hall in Goatstown had been purchased and renovated at a cost of about eight thousand pounds. It was a large two-storey building, with seventeen rooms and garden space, and had been secured only after an extensive search of the Dublin property market. Valerie remembers feeling that they would never have to move again, as Prospect Hall appeared so large after the cramped conditions in Pembroke Street. 'Until Major Beaumont came on the scene, I think we were at a bit of a dead end. I was wondering was this as far as I could go. But his offer to double whatever we could raise towards a new building came out of the blue. Things moved quickly then. But before we took Goatstown we looked at a house in Dundrum which I rather liked. After we expressed an interest in buying the house, the owner told someone from the clinic that he wasn't going to have people coming into Dundrum spreading germs. When Kathleen heard about it she was incensed as I was. I tried to talk to him and explain that our children would be convalescent patients but he wouldn't listen. I think that kind of attitude is interesting because it shows how terrified people were of polio. There was no cure and so it frightened them.

'In the end we were delighted with Goatstown. I was flabbergasted with the size at first. There was so much space. We put in a lift and made the rooms suitable for the doctors and physios, and for the first time people were not all jumbled up together. I even had a room of my own. Then we got our own van. It had three wheels and was a gift from a sheet-metal company in Howth. Kathleen used to drive that; unfortunately it turned over with her in it, but she was all right. From then on things began to be run more efficiently. We realised that it was becoming impossible to operate the driving end of things on a completely voluntary basis, and we employed our first professional driver. The voluntary aspect of the clinic has always been very important, but in order to provide a proper professional service people had to be paid. One of the reasons we had such great physiotherapists was that we paid them on the English Whitley scale, which meant that we were able to attract the best staff. But we were also terribly lucky with the calibre of person who came to help. Look at people like Dr James Hanlon. He was a leading Dublin eye, nose and throat surgeon who lost his sight and hearing around 1950. He went off to England and trained as a physiotherapist and came back to work for the clinic. He was quite remarkable. He used the only facility he had left, his sense of touch, in order to make himself useful. He was great. He travelled to America with me on one of our fundraising visits there, and appeared on the Ed Sullivan show. I remember that after the show we all said that we would go to a nightclub and Jim said he'd come. He said that even though he couldn't see or hear he could feel the beat and the rhythm.

He just hadn't given up. In the end he died in Lourdes, which was exactly where he had always said he wanted to die.'

A look at the chairman's report for the period April 1956/7 provides a good insight into the progress made in the six years since Valerie and Kathleen had first opened the doors at Pembroke Street. The flag days made a net profit of over three thousand pounds, while an appearance by Noël Coward at the opening dance of the new Shelbourne Hotel ballroom netted over six hundred and thirty pounds profit. The fact that the staff from the clinic did a lot more than just their work, is obvious from the fact that the physiotherapists managed to collect twenty-three pounds when Chipperfield's Circus allowed them to pass the CRC box during the show. In June the clinic established a pension scheme, while in October a school was started, with the Department of Education providing a teacher. The number of patients treated continued to rise, with one hundred and seventy-nine seen during the period, eighty-one of whom were new. In July the CRC was asked to send some of its physiotherapists to Cork to help with the latest outbreak of poliomyelitis there. The fact that the request was made, and that the clinic was able to respond, shows that even at that early stage it was held in high esteem.

Despite that high esteem, Dublin's archbishop, John Charles McQuaid, refused to cooperate when Valerie asked him to be associated with the clinic. Geraldine Cruess-Callaghan remembers Valerie's disappointment very well. 'She wasn't a Catholic at that stage but she wanted the archbishop involved in some way, either on the board or as a patron. She wrote to him in the proper fashion when Goatstown had been purchased. She got a reply saying that it wasn't his policy to belong to something unless it was 100 per cent Catholic. The point was of course that almost everybody except Valerie was Catholic. I think it did hurt her a bit. Afterwards when she converted she wondered whether she should write and ask him then but I don't think she did.'

Valerie's determination to improve the clinic's facilities was never hindered by a lack of money. She began badgering her committee and trustees about building a hydrotherapy pool before they had time to congratulate themselves on the move to Goatstown. In February 1955, barely a month after the new clinic had been officially opened by

President Seán T O'Kelly, Valerie was selling her swimming-pool scheme to her more cautious governors. She argued that if the CRC was ahead of the rest of the twenty-six counties in providing a pool, then the clinic would benefit from the fact that hydrotherapy training was being made compulsory for physiotherapists, who would utilise the pool as part of their studies. On this occasion Valerie was given the go-ahead to discuss the issue with the minister for health. A year and a half later, in September 1957, the governors agreed that the swimming-pool project could begin when four thousand pounds had been set aside for the purpose. But in the end Valerie had to wait until the beginning of 1959 before she was able to give the all-clear to the construction company. In the meantime, all kinds of fundraising activities had been undertaken, including the sale of cardboard tiles designed to look like the tiles that cover the walls of a swimming pool. 'In fundraising you have to do something very specific. People must be able to see exactly where their money is going. And by buying the mock tiles, people felt that they were actually building a bit of the pool themselves.'

> The chairman of the Central Remedial Clinic, Lady Goulding, said that the opening of the pool had been made possible only by the hard work of so many people. Referring to the committees who had worked so hard on behalf of the clinic, Lady Goulding said: 'This pool may not look big, and the sum of £10,000 enormous, but afterwards, when you will look back and see our gigantic heating and purification installation, then you will realise where the money went. I am unable to thank you adequately, though I wish to do so most sincerely. However, I think your best thanks will be when I tell you the true story of one of our patients. For the past three years this patient has been unable to walk without the aid of crutches and callipers. This week, for the first time, in the pool, she walked unaided. It was all of you who helped with the flag-selling, running fetes and sales of work, and many other tedious ways of raising funds, who gave such joy'.[11]

Valerie's speech on the day that the pool was officially opened is an example of what she was best at. Kay Keating, who was chief superintendent physiotherapist at the clinic for many years, calls it Valerie's 'Ra Ra' quality. Taking off Valerie's perfect English tones, Kay describes her gathering 'all the troops together and telling us all that we were one big happy family. She had this great capacity for rallying people'. It is what Tony O'Reilly calls Valerie's 'Raj' factor. Valerie knew how to lead her army into battle. And when the battle was over, she knew that the troops needed commendation.

As the range of services provided at Goatstown grew, the numbers seeking treatment there rocketed. Apart from the addition of the pool, a training workshop was built in 1964, while the need for greater educational facilities was becoming critical. By the mid 1960s it was clear that the time to move on had come, and once again Valerie's connections saved the day. George Ansley of Ansbacher Bank had known Walter Monckton and had arranged to have dinner with Basil and Valerie while he was visiting Dublin in the late 1960s. During dinner he spoke about the horrific death of his daughter Penny and her daughter in a motor accident. Not knowing anything about Valerie's work, he asked her how she spent her time. When she explained that she was in the middle of trying to raise funds for a new clinic, he told her that he had been thinking of donating money to a charity in honour of his daughter. Valerie recollects that on the morning after the dinner he rang her and asked her to come straight away and show him the proposed new clinic. Mr Ansley was impressed and promised to help. However, as Geraldine Cruess-Callaghan remembers, Mr Ansley promised one hundred thousand pounds, with three conditions.

'Valerie met him around the time of the move to Clontarf when we were desperately trying to raise funds. He promised the money on the basis that the new building would be called after his daughter, Penny. He also would have very much liked to have been given the freedom of the city of Dublin and he also wanted the government to match his financial contribution. Well, calling the building after Penny was no problem and we got the money from the government, but despite Valerie's efforts it was impossible to arrange the freedom of the city. We were very disappointed about it all and quite desperate for the cash. So I said let's head over to Paris and see if we can meet him and explain the situation. When we got there Valerie rang him and asked him to lunch. She didn't say that we were there just to see him, but made it sound casual. He said he'd love to see us for lunch and suggested Maxim's. We got there early and had the bucket of champagne ready and we were making a great fuss, hoping to impress him. When he arrived he appeared so tiny. He was just over an operation and he was neither able to drink the champagne nor eat his lunch. I think his stomach was gone. But we started talking and he was so gracious. He said how nice it was that two pretty ladies had come to Paris to see him. I told him that we had wanted to give him champagne to prepare him for the good news and the bad news. We told him that we could fulfil the conditions except the freedom of the city. Before the lunch was over Valerie told him directly why we had come and he said that he was not going to let us down. He agreed to the one hundred thousand pounds there and then.' Valerie remembers that unfortunately in their enthusiasm they rushed out of Maxim's without paying the bill.

President de Valera opened the new clinic at Vernon Avenue in Clontarf in 1968. George Ansley was there and was, as Valerie remembers, delighted to meet the president. The new building was designed by Michael Scott, who was a good friend of the Gouldings. At the time it was regarded as both a medical and architectural showpiece. It cost around five hundred thousand pounds to build and equip, four-fifths of which came from voluntary subscriptions. With the building of Clontarf and the subsequent increase in the number of patients treated, Valerie became more and more convinced of the need for bigger and greater fundraising events. Many of these occasions were major public relations exercises, but today many people, including those who admire her, question the actual financial value of some of her favourite events. A perfect example of this clash of opinion is provided by the Jimmy Saville walks, which began in 1967.

There must have been 25,000 people in that joyous explosion of Dubliners. Long before 10.30am they were streaming into Abbey Street, swirling into an ever-growing torrent around the platform outside the *Herald* office. On the platform the music of an outfit known as The Clouds was filling the street with its pulsating throb. The young revellers beat their hands in time to it.

Suddenly the crowd was convulsed by a series of yells. Cause of the hysteria was James Mason, who came from the inner gloom of the *Herald* office and walked out into the brilliant morning sunshine.

He was followed by Dickie Rock, the 'Duchess' (Jimmy Saville's wonderful mother), and Lady Goulding, looking well after her hepatitis. She was all set for Baldoyle in green wind-cheater and slacks.

Next came Chris Curran, Charles Mitchell and Pat Taaffe. All were engulfed in ear splitting welcomes. Then it started. 'WE WANT JIMMY!' And they got him. Jimmy has a habit of appearing with the swiftness of the Demon in a panto.

The morning breeze blowing his blonde hair all over his face and shoulders, he tore off his track suit and stood revealed in white shorts. Nothing else.[12]

At first glance it is difficult to conjure up a more unlikely combination than Lady Valerie Goulding and Jimmy Saville. 'I did genuinely love him. He's extremely funny and he used to say the most ghastly things. I liked him because he was genuine. After the walks he often came to see the children in the clinic. They loved it and he really did love the children.' Perhaps Valerie's affection for Jimmy is not so hard to understand when one considers that Jimmy Saville's eccentricity was very similar to Basil's: both men often wore funny clothes, played practical jokes, and enjoyed slapstick humour. Valerie had been introduced to Jimmy through the editor of the *Sunday People*. 'In the late sixties when we were trying to get the funds together to move the clinic from Goatstown, I realised that I needed to get out of the stream of people that I was always asking for help. Gilbert Harding of the *Sunday People* used to send us a contribution at Christmas time and I asked him if he had any ideas. He told me to come over and meet his secretary who could organise a meeting with Jimmy Saville. At that stage I thought, Jimmy who? When I went over to London I invited him to lunch. I met him at an Italian restaurant and he looked just awful.

'We sat down and it was terrible because neither of us was saying anything. Jimmy said to me "I wonder which of us is more frightened of the other. Because I'm certainly frightened of you". So I said let's talk about something close to my heart and asked him to do an appeal. As he was leaving he asked if we had ever had sponsored walks in Ireland. I thought it sounded like a great idea and it hadn't been done. So he said that if I arranged everything on my end that he would come over and do a ten-mile walk. He said that he wanted to be put up in the Gresham and that he wanted to be met from the boat by a Rolls Royce. Well, he came and it was great. There were thousands of people waiting outside the *Independent* in Abbey Street for the start, but Jimmy slipped out the back door, so only the good runners could keep up with him. Many people were involved and it was really a great crush. The drinkers from the Yacht pub in Clontarf acted as bodyguards. I can't tell you how many people came along, both famous and friends of the clinic. Of course the entire staff, including the physios, would turn out. Everybody was involved. And after the first one Jimmy and I discussed it and he said he would come back and we did it for years afterwards. It maddens me now to think of how all these other charities have used our ideas. I know that's the wrong feeling but when the other walks started we didn't make as much. Jimmy was still a pull but the crowds weren't as big.'

Valerie sees the late 1960s and 1970s as the high-water mark of her fundraising activities. 'Bing Crosby came over and spoke at a dinner for us. He wasn't keen on doing a radio appeal but he said that he would speak. He stayed with Raymond Guest who was the American ambassador at the time. I remember he told all the people who turned up that night that they were in an expensive hotel and that they should put their hands in their pockets and donate a hundred pounds. Then he said "here's mine". There was silence. He wasn't as great a talker as you'd think. But he was very relaxed when he came to Dargle for lunch with his new wife. I wish he'd been more relaxed at the dance. I suppose it wasn't one of our best fundraisers but it was great from the PR point of view. It was all over the papers. Then of course there was the Bal Des Petits Lits Blancs that was held here in 1965. I think that I got in touch with Princess Grace through Lord Killanin, as he was the consul for Monaco. She agreed to come if we split the proceeds between us and a charity of her choice. Then I asked Mrs Slazenger if she would allow us to use Powerscourt House for the night and she agreed. Charlie was minister for health at that time, and he came out to the airport to meet Princess Grace and Prince Rainier. I remember that everyone was very jealous of Basil because she spent the afternoon with him in his box at Fitzwilliam looking at the tennis because we had a big tournament on. You know, afterwards he told me that he'd had an awful time because he couldn't get a word out of her. One awful thing happened just before she came down to eat at the ball. Somebody went in and upturned the table at which she was going to have dinner.

Everything went all over the place. We were so busy trying to get it back together that we forgot to find out who did it. But they didn't know anything had happened. Prince Rainier was very sweet and Princess Grace danced with lots of people. We got huge coverage.'

Hugh Robinson, who worked for the CRC for over thirty years, justifies the high profile and high cost of many of Valerie's favourite fundraisers. He argues that the clinic often benefited in an indirect way long after the event was over. He points out that it was through Baron Sellier, one of the key organisers of the Bal Des Petits Lits Blancs, that Valerie made contact with George Ansley who had donated so generously to the Clontarf building fund. Essentially Robinson's argument is that while the events in themselves did not always raise a huge amount of funds, they raised the clinic's profile, which in turn helped to generate money. Ken Holden, who took over from Valerie when she retired in 1980, feels that she found it difficult to accept that some of her ideas were no longer good money-spinners. 'I think she was unwilling to recognise that the events that she loved and that she had created with all their colour and glamour – especially the Jimmy Saville walk in its final days – that it wasn't justified in terms of the money raised. Questions could have been raised had the figures been made public. She felt that they were justified because of the image that was generated. It was potentially dangerous to raise people's expectations through these events. I think that the problem was that she was willing to take on new ideas but she was reluctant to let go of the old ones.'

Another factor in the difference of opinion over the value of the high profile events is the fact that some clinic employees felt that Valerie tended to look at the gross intake and often failed to quantify the real cost involved. On the other hand critics would admit that engaging in large publicity-pulling ventures made it easier to draw funds from the State. Talking to some of the people who have worked with Valerie over the years, it is clear that they believe that her attitude to many of the issues involved in fundraising has not moved with the changed status of the clinic. While many acknowledge that in the 1950s and 1960s she made disability acceptable by glamorising it, they feel that she has not come to terms with the reality of the dominant role now played by government in the management of society's health and social needs.

Close friends like Geraldine Cruess-Callaghan admit that it appears difficult for Valerie to come to terms with the clinic as it is run today but she emphasises that nobody could beat Valerie when it came to identifying people who could help the clinic.

Perhaps one of her shrewdest moves was to ask Charles Haughey to head a fundraising committee in the immediate aftermath of the Arms Trial.[13] Valerie is open about the fact that she perceived the Haughey move as a straightforward trade-off between his money-making ability for the clinic and his need to involve himself in activities that would help his political rehabilitation in the wake of his arrest, trial and sacking from the government. 'I didn't want to know if he was or wasn't involved in arms. I never discussed the North with him. I just talked to him about the clinic. I guessed that if he stayed doing clinic-type activities then it would help him back into power. It probably sounds rather nasty but it was good for the clinic. So many people hated him at the time but I suppose he realised that working for the clinic would help in terms of his public acceptability.' Mr Haughey says that he didn't agree straight away to Valerie's proposal. 'I told her that I would stir up certain resentments. But she said she wanted me very definitely and so I went ahead. First thing I did was to go off to see the bank people on College Green. I'd been led to believe that they were going to close the clinic but they were a pushover. I told them about our plan to raise money and they accepted it. So she was very pleased – she always is when she gets her own way. We organised a committee and weekly meetings. We used to have them in that awful atrocity of a building on the canal – Basil's building, Fitzwilton.'

As Valerie remembers it, about eight people were involved in the planning meetings headed by Mr Haughey. 'We met on a Tuesday for three-quarters of an hour. That was all Charlie would allow. The idea was that everyone was given a task and Charlie would go around the table during the meeting looking for everyone's report.' Geraldine Cruess-Callaghan was on the committee and says that Mr Haughey imbued everyone with a sense of not wanting to fail. 'He'd ask you what you had got in that week and you just wanted to be able to answer positively. He was great and there were just so many people beholden to him. He'd roped in a lot of help, businessmen and henchmen.'

According to Valerie, Mr Haughey's committee had promises of three hundred thousand pounds before they even set out for the United States on their speaking tour. 'I told him I was happy but he said he had promised us fifty thousand pounds more than that, and that is what we would get.'

Geraldine always kept a diary when they travelled so that she'd know who to write thank you letters to afterwards. 'We went out to America on Easter Saturday 1972. Toddy and Niamh O'Sullivan from the Gresham Hotel came with us. Kevin McClory didn't travel because he was out there. He had made a great film about the clinic and we were going to use that as part of the tour. We had reserved seats at a High Mass in St Patrick's Cathedral in New York on the Sunday and we then had a private meeting with Cardinal Cooke. I even have a note here that says that Toddy paid for our lunch at Reubens. Our American committees were going well then. The best one was in Boston and was run by Florence McGarrity. She worked in banking there and was really dedicated to the clinic. It is a pity that Florence wasn't involved in some of the earlier trips because some of them could have been better organised. Toddy was managing director of the Gresham and was able to get free rooms for us in the Plaza Hotel. What we basically did was show Kevin's film and afterwards Charlie would make a speech and then Valerie would talk and see if we could get subscriptions. Charlie never talked about politics on that trip. He used to tell the gathering all about Valerie and how she'd come over to Ireland and had started this great work. I suppose he was getting a great image out of the involvement.' Mr Haughey says that they went down well with the Americans. 'They'd call her Lady Val. It was a bit of an old gimmick and I was able to open up a lot of doors for her in the Irish-American community. But it wasn't easy. It was a little disappointing. They weren't rushing at us with money. It was a hard slog but we did have good fun: we were in my favourite hotel – the Plaza.'

In the mid 1960s, following the development of the Salk vaccine and the subsequent successful nationwide immunisation programme, poliomyelitis was brought under control, but it soon became clear to people like Doctor Boyd Dunlop as well as others in the clinic, that there were many other conditions requiring specialised services.

J Boyd Dunlop encouraged Valerie to look for another medical director with a wider experience in the treatment of cerebral palsy, spina bifida, muscular dystrophy and other congenital conditions. The arrival of Dr Ciaran Barry was the start of what Doctor Dunlop calls 'an explosion of activities'. Máirín Byrne, who has been responsible for much of the developments in the area of educational services at the clinic, echoes the huge admiration felt at the CRC for Dr Barry's pioneering work. 'Ciaran Barry was from Donegal and in the early 1960s he was working in London as the senior registrar in the Department of Physical Medicine in Guy's Hospital. He was also a consultant to the National Spastic Society. He was a man of hybrid abilities. Lady Goulding went over to see him after his name was suggested to her, and while he was anxious to return to Dublin, he wanted a consultant's post and he wasn't prepared to give up his position in London without having a secure position here. In the end he was offered a consultancy post in the Mater Hospital on a half-time basis and a half-time position here. When he finally came in 1964, he had a much broader understanding of handicap than just polio. His whole approach was to offer greater and broader services at the clinic. In a sense the clinic was nothing more than the outpatient unit of a hospital between 1951 and 1964, but between then and 1976 when the CRC was taken in under the Department of Health, there was tremendous progress. I think that because Dr Barry was just back from London, there was a great aura about him. He really did have a great vision of the service that he wanted to provide. By 1968 the profile of people being treated at the CRC had completely changed, as had the services that were being provided.'

It is clear from any conversation with staff at the clinic that Dr Barry is held in the highest esteem: it is also clear that Valerie is acknowledged as playing a role in attracting people of calibre who would help give the clinic the reputation it has today. Some people, including current and former members of staff, feel however that while Valerie had 'no hesitation in selecting great people, she had difficulties dealing with them when they became bigger than her. In some ways it was as if she came to resent them'.[14] If such difficulties did exist, there seems to be no doubt that Valerie had a good relationship with Dr Barry, who always made a point of explaining medical developments to her. The CRC's former chief superintendent physiotherapist, Kay Keating, points out that Dr Barry 'had a great understanding of Lady Goulding. He never allowed her to feel sidelined. She didn't hear things that she might want to have been a part of from junior members of staff because he made a point of telling her first. He made sure that she was included in the decision-making process'. It is difficult for any individual to watch as the product of their effort and imagination grows beyond them. And perhaps because Valerie's effort had been on such a grand scale she faced a more daunting task than most.

From the late 1960s on, the scale of operation at the CRC bore no comparison with its beginnings in a small flat on Upper Pembroke Street. It was ahead of its time in the development of many electronics-based resources which helped to transform the lives of many handicapped people, including award-winning writer Christopher Nolan. Ken Holden argues against the criticism of some of the medical people who would feel that Valerie was unwise to single Christopher out. 'Her support of Christopher Nolan was controversial. But the use of computers and the work that evolved from that for other children probably wouldn't have happened without the single-minded support that she gave to Christopher. There were reservations in the beginning from some of the medical people, but then medical people never like promoting individual patients, but Valerie just single-mindedly said "let's promote him". As I saw it, Christopher's success highlighted two things. Firstly that there were people of great handicap who could be a Shakespeare, and secondly it showed the potential for helping such people. The immediacy of Christopher's triumph was much better than an abstract paper in ten years' time and she saw that. I do believe that she moved with the times. She understood and was able to move forward from the treatment of polio to cerebral palsy. But within the clinic there was always going to be a conflict between Valerie's desire to make people put their hands in their pockets and the medical view that it should be presented in a more abstract way.'

Christopher Nolan gives us a glimpse of the Valerie he knew in his book, *Under the Eye of the Clock*:

Like the school, the founder was Hector-hearted. Joseph[15] had seen her on one of his visits to the clinic, but when the classroom door flew open one day, he failed to recognise the lady who blustered in. She was dressed in a paisley design, mustard-coloured dress and flat shoes. 'Good afternoon Lady Goulding', chorused the pupils. 'Good afternoon children', smiled the visitor. She stood talking with the teacher while Joseph sat looking at none other than Lady Valerie Goulding.

Hesitating at the door she smiled at the class and in a fluster she was gone. Her fact remained before his mind's eye, her trestled truth shone from her gaze, her smile came from a soul-burst and he remembered that she had had a ladder in her stocking.[16]

Apart from the medical, scientific and service developments that Valerie had to accommodate, she also had to come to terms with the changing nature of how society dealt with the treatment and rehabilitation of handicapped people. When Ken Holden took over from Valerie in 1980, the CRC was in the middle of a move away from a voluntary organisation to an essentially State-funded service. 'Clearly society was changing, but there was a threat that the clinic would end up as a totally State-dominated service. I believed in the American view that the best way of providing services is through a combination of State and voluntary sector involvement. When I arrived the clinic desperately needed to make the transition from the voluntary to the professional era, and it needed someone who could make that bridge. My first task was to stabilise the balance sheet while preserving the integrity of the spirit of the place. I was afraid that Valerie wouldn't give me the degree of latitude I needed, but I must say that with very few exceptions she did. It was a good combination and we did work well together. She was very good at motivating people. She was a leader. Everyone thinks that her only role was fundraising: she wasn't all that spectacularly successful as a fundraiser but she was spectacularly successful at motivating people. She was of the girl-guide variety. She believed in motivating people and then leaving them to do their own thing. I was there when the place was experiencing great change. I would not have wanted to be part of something that wasn't crusading. But as it changed it was inevitable that it was going to end up as a nine-to-five thing for most people, and she bitterly resented that.' As Máirín Byrne emphasises, the up-side of Valerie's early style of running the clinic was that it wasn't run like a health board. 'We were able to get equipment and things that we needed. I remember that Kay Keating had facilities that nobody else in the country had. Money was the chief difference then, and in Lady Goulding's early days she had an incredible ability to generate finance.'

The question that most rapidly springs to mind in any consideration of Valerie's achievement is what motivated her to dedicate her entire life to this cause. Her friend Tony O'Reilly feels that she has many of the qualities that Mrs Thatcher displays. 'She has a strong sense of purposefulness. She believes in self-reliance and has a sense of responsibility towards others. She was never shy about using what she was. In Ireland she represented a sort of limited nobility and she used it. She has a great streak of generosity, and then there was the nanny factor. Valerie knew how to motivate people to get things done, and although she believed in self-reliance she embraced government. She almost deified Charlie Haughey because she thought he personified a caring government and was a generous man, albeit with government funds. Fundamentally, she believed that it was the private purpose of life to be charitable and helpful, and with her English sense of purposefulness she went straight for the line.'

Ken Holden feels that 'in retrospect people sometimes assign too much thinking' to an issue like personal motivation. 'She would say herself that she was horrified by what she saw of the polio epidemic here in the 1950s. But she was probably also at a loose end. She had wanted to be a doctor and perhaps it was easier to express her emotions through her work for the clinic than it was for her to express them in a close personal relationship. It is singularly difficult to get close to Valerie. There are layers and layers there. Geraldine Cruess-Callaghan is the only person that I know who is close.' Geraldine argues that there was 'an urge in Valerie to do something which was to the exclusion of everyone and everything else. Her boys went to boarding school very early and she had to do something'.

When one asks Valerie to explain her motivation she tends to remember the horrible injuries that she witnessed during the war, the poverty and illness on the streets of Dublin in the 1940s and 1950s, and individual images of human degradation. 'I remember being told that there was a child in a terrible state somewhere in Galway. As we often camped down in Clifden, I made a point of calling to the house where I was told the child was. I said to the mother when I got there that I'd heard that one of her children was ill, but she said that they were all fine. So I started to walk back out through the kitchen. Then I saw what I first thought was a dog on the floor, eating from a bowl. I was stunned because the dog was a child on all fours. The child was completely crippled. But nobody was saying anything because one didn't admit to having TB or polio. The poor child was filthy and he smelt. I went back to the mother and said that I might be able to help. But it really was the first time since the war that I had seen anyone in such a terrible state. The child was hardly human.'

'An assessment of the contribution she has made is simple. Without her there would be no clinic.' Ken Holden acknowledges the criticism that can be laid at Valerie's door but argues that her achievements supersede her faults. 'When you needed something Valerie was the one to get it: whether it was a political favour or whatever, she could cajole people, bully people, and above all get them.' For Kay Keating she is a woman 'who has great courage: who was prepared to go into great debt and who was not afraid to ask people like George Ansley for the money she needed. She was a good fundraiser up until the 1970s. And she was wise to hand over in 1980'. For Doctor Boyd Dunlop her legacy is simply that 'there would have been no clinic without her. If I'd been alone there wouldn't have been a clinic: if Kathleen had been alone there wouldn't have been a clinic, but if Valerie had been alone she would have gathered the people around her who would have made it possible. I do believe that it took her to get it going'.

Robert Kelly was one of the many children who travelled across the city for treatment at the Goatstown clinic.

Dear Lady Goulding,

I would like to thank you for the lovely day you gave my family and I at the Central Remedial Clinic. I can't express how much I was looking forward to seeing you. I was also looking forward to thanking you personally for the lovely memories I have of you and the happy times I had at the Central Remedial Clinic in Goatstown.

The journey we had from Ballyfermot to Goatstown in the three-wheeled van is a picture that remains very clear in my head. The smell of petrol and the one window which I think six of us used to try to look out of. (I never knew where Goatstown was because I could never see where I was going.) Also I remember swimming at Tara Street Baths every Friday morning . . . . I remember with great fondness your own personal kindness to me. The time you took me to your own home, and your three boxer dogs. The time you brought me scrambling. The occasion that you came to my home with presents and food for my family at Christmas.

Dear Lady Goulding thank you once again for your kindness.[17]

Billy Sugrue was six months old when he contracted polio. As a very young child he was operated on by Dr Boyd Dunlop. 'My very first recollection is going up a very long winding staircase with Lady Goulding and Kathleen O'Rourke. I don't suppose I knew what was going on. Kathleen used to come out to my house in Finglas even on a Saturday to give me therapy. I had so many 'ops' that I missed a lot of the Pembroke days, but when I got out it had moved to Goatstown. I had to get intensive physiotherapy as I was affected in my arms, legs and trunk. I remember the only time that Kathleen was strict was when she was treating me. If I hadn't had that physiotherapy I would be finished. Lady Goulding was always there. There was never any act with her. She'd always chat no matter where you were and it wasn't just for the public. Every year when she went on her holidays she used to send me a card from Switzerland. She used to call me Billy William. She brought me home to Dargle and I met the boys, Tim and Ham. They used to call me Boss because I was always saying what I wanted. I wouldn't trade places in my life: the clinic has looked after me from day one. It gave me an education and in the end it gave me a job and now I'm married with two daughters. Lady G didn't care where the money came from and I think she was right. As far as I'm concerned nobody has the right to criticise her, but I can see how it happens. I never saw her cross or down. The impression I got was that she was very defensive about the clinic and she was a great fighter. She deserves all the praise she can get for what she has done. She should be honoured. I suppose her biggest skill is that you could never say no to her. Now I get the impression that she is frustrated and would like to transfer her brain into a younger body.'

1 *The Irish Times*, 29 June 1951.

2 Minutes of the inaugural meeting of the trustees, 1 May 1951.

3 Minutes of the second meeting of the Dublin Remedial Clinic.

4 *The Irish Times*, 7 March 1952.

5 Valerie to Basil, 14 March 1952. 'Pie' was one of Basil's pet names for Valerie; UDH was shorthand for an American family.

6 Valerie to Basil, undated.

7 Valerie to Basil, 30 March 1952.

8 Minutes of clinic trustees meeting, 20 July 1952.

9 Meeting of clinic trustees meeting, 27 October 1952.

10 Major Michael Wentworth Beaumont of Harristown House, Brannockstown, County Kildare.

11 *The Irish Times*, 19 July 1961.

12 *Evening Herald*, 4 May 1970.

13 In May 1970 the Taoiseach, Jack Lynch, dismissed Charles Haughey and Neil Blaney from his cabinet following allegations that there had been a conspiracy to supply arms to the IRA. They were arrested and charged with conspiracy to import arms and ammunition into the State. There was insufficient evidence against Blaney and Haughey was found not guilty. Charles Haughey succeeded Jack Lynch as leader of Fianna Fáil in 1979.

14 Senior former member of staff.

15 Christopher called himself 'Joseph' in his book.

16 *Under the Eye of the Clock*. Picador, 1990.

17 Robert Kelly to Lady Goulding, 11 October 1992.

6

LIFE AT DARGLE COTTAGE

The score of 28 years is so impressive that one has the feeling that it must be a record. And certainly I think it very likely so – if you take into account both the positives of pleasure and the negatives of acrimony.

The only frightening thing about it, I sometimes think, is the tendency to take it for granted – such as by forgetting our anniversary!

Indeed I do believe that your absence for the last month makes the pleasure keener: and the prospect of your return in another adds edge.

Russell Murphy[1] said the other evening, how he found the family a contented one; and that comment from outside at once underlined for me your magnetic force toward this effect . . . .

I have to (ooze ?) off to Fitzwilliam now: but not before sounding-off an inadequate bouquet of verbal thanks with a big verbal orchid on top for being such a beautiful wife and mistress for so long.[2]

For many of their contemporaries Basil and Valerie Goulding were an odd couple. Odd, because unlike many marriages neither partner's identity was lost in the coupling: odd, also, because each led a separate and independent life and appeared not to need the imprimatur of the other. Typically, while critics use kind and interesting words such as 'eccentric' or 'dilettante' when describing Basil, Valerie is sometimes criticised because she allegedly wasn't a good home-maker. Had a man achieved all that Valerie has, it is doubtful if questions would be asked about whether he was a good housekeeper and it is only in recent times that he would face questions about the quality of his family life. In more ways than one, Valerie was ahead of her time. In her public achievement she displayed both the charitable intuition of the class and generation from which she came, as well as the entrepreneurial and public relations skills that would be the byword for success in Lemass's Ireland. But what made Valerie an easy target for people who expected a woman to behave like a woman should, was the fact that from her perspective, she was doing exactly what she had been brought up to do: it would never have occurred to her to think that cooking a dinner should be the yardstick of her success as a human being. Valerie is no feminist: she simply does not like work in the kitchen, and as the typical product of an upper-class English household she had no expectation that she would ever have to linger much below stairs.

Basil wrote the letter, quoted above, to Valerie on their twenty-eighth wedding anniversary. Apart from the obvious tenderness of its tone, there is a palpable sense of passion in his reference to her being 'such a beautiful wife and mistress for so long'. Basil's letters are always emotionally and sexually expressive, and are in stark contrast to the tightness of his personal dealings with both friends and family. Geraldine Cruess-Callaghan remembers Basil's distaste at seeing a young couple dance closely. He told her that 'that sort of thing was best kept for the bedroom'. To the outside world Basil was either a madman or a genius, full of fun and pranks, and always the centre of attention: very few people got a glimpse of the man that Valerie loved.

> I get so excited sometimes now at the thought of soon being able to hug and kiss my beautiful girlfriend again. I don't know how I've lasted out so long without her. By the way, I must show you some rather amusing evidence of the strain!
>
> Loads of Wog's best affection to you. I'm glad you say I wasn't as much trouble, as a patient, as I might have been; but I'm sure I was quite enough. And you my darling were always so attentive, and so non-fratchy in spite of Sally, that you contributed a whole lot to the long hibernation. Anyhow, at the start of another Spring my fancy lightly turns to the same dear love with no qualms about her being other than the best in the world.[3]

There is a sense of slight regret and emotional turmoil when Valerie talks about Basil, who died in 1982. Talking about him, she emphasises his perfectness, and while denying that the marriage was ever in trouble, she attributes any failings there might have been to herself. Reading Basil's letters one could presume that Valerie was the most important event in his life. And yet she is not sure. 'I would like to say that I was the most important thing in Basil's life, but I don't know. We had no crisis – forty-three years and no crisis. We were always physically in love – even in our sixties – until he was ill. We had a very strong sexual relationship. But I think that he was less in love with me than I was with him. I admired him so much. He had everything: he was intellectual, loved laughter, and was good looking.'

Tim Goulding's ex-wife, Annie,[4] loved Basil and Valerie dearly. When Basil was dying of cancer, both she and Tim came to Dargle to be with him in his last months. Annie, who like Tim is an artist and also a great cook, is a shy and sensitive person possessed of a somewhat mystical quality. She points out that the age difference between Basil and Valerie would have had an effect on the way their relationship operated. 'Remember that when they married she was ten years younger. She was in awe of him, and he was already running his business, in a position of power and control. Patterns of behaviour set in youth continue, and Valerie's involvement in the clinic probably prevented her from being overshadowed. She could have been swamped otherwise. Basil would have been very difficult to live with. He was very demanding, had very high standards, and had overall control of everything. Her room in Dargle was very much her domain. She had special things from her family there – lovely pieces of furniture, some favourite paintings and a writing desk. It was a unit on its own, and I feel she must have needed that space because the rest of the house was very much Basil's domain.'

It is interesting that Valerie's sons do not regard the separateness and independence of their parents' lives as a problem, though some older members of Basil's coterie feel that he suffered because of Valerie's commitments. 'They were two complete opposites. They had so little in common that they had almost completely different lives. I don't think there was a home life. He'd go home and there was no dinner. They were both strong personalities, and while I don't think that he was an unhappy man, I think that there were certain elements of happiness that he didn't enter into in his life.'[5] Ham Goulding takes a completely opposite view. 'People wonder what kept them together. Maybe it was that very diversity, because on the surface they appear to have little in common except the project of creating a home and kids, but neither of them were tied to that as a concept.' Tim agrees that his mother and father were far apart in terms of their thoughts and interests, but he feels that 'the man and woman physical attraction was very strong. That's what held them together'. Some of Basil's friends display a stereotyped idea of the qualities that a woman should bring to a marriage. 'I think that if they'd been running a normal house it wouldn't have worked. She was totally undomesticated, with no interest in the garden or the house, and she couldn't cook. Basil said that she had other attributes. He told me that he preferred to do the garden and the house anyway. I think that he would have appreciated it had she learned to cook. There were always different people coming and going in the kitchen. He was so good at so many things that she'd be less good at. He was always redecorating. I think that she was ninety-five percent wrapped up in the clinic, more than her home or her children or anything.'

Basil's letters to Valerie when she was travelling abroad to raise funds for the clinic give no hint of this alleged dissatisfaction: there is nothing but a sense of longing in Basil's prose:

> Don't you think, Darling that you could call it a day pretty quickly now? You're such a main delight to me that I'm getting a bit derelict from your long absence. It doesn't I find, make the heart grow fonder anymore, after a few days, because mine has already run up against the reading which says 'Full'.
>
> By the way – and this is asked so casually that you'd hardly notice it as having any interest! – how will the Calendar be operating at the time you get back? I only asked, mind, because I'm a bit short of news; but will it be alright, yes?
>
> I hope all the lovely Americans are appreciating their treat in meeting you and seeing your lovely elegant beauty. At any rate I'm getting jealous of them and a little impatient for a big squeeze and such a kissing-over as never was.[6]

In retrospect, Valerie muses a little about the domestic side of their life. 'I always feel badly about the fact that maybe he wanted a good housewife. I couldn't cook or wash up. I just didn't like that side of life, and perhaps he would have liked a nice quiet housewife. But he didn't marry one. I think opposites are good things. We didn't have rows. He went silent for two days if he was annoyed about something. Even though we had cooks and maids, Basil would ask if I'd seen the dust on this or that. Then after the silence he'd realise that it didn't really matter. Doing things was the best time for us. He'd garden at weekends, and of course the camping and the skiing was great fun when we were all together. My migraine affected me a lot and when I had a headache I did tell him to go out without me, and he did. He was probably out as much as I was, but we did go to a lot of places separately. I think I do regret that I wasn't a better housewife. It's almost as if I was another generation from his. I think that he felt I should be a good housewife as well as doing the work that I did. I remember the time when I'd got the very first van for the clinic and I brought it home here, but he never mentioned it for two days and then he said "jolly good". I think that if I'd gone into the kitchen and made a good dinner he'd have been much happier. He was probably a little jealous of my time in the clinic. Women in those days played cards, bridge or something. I did go to the business lunches with him if I had to, but I was bored by the business because he never spoke about it except when there was trouble.' Valerie's friend Brenda Clarke feels that she never left the big house and the era of servants. 'Many of us lived in those big houses and we didn't do anything, but we did have to learn – Valerie didn't.'

Valerie and Basil lived at a time when families from their background were beginning to learn how to live without a large retinue. But when they set up house in Dargle in 1946, they employed a nanny, cook, parlour-maid, nursery maid and gardener, as well as some casual men who helped with the outside work. With this lifestyle came the expectation of a public school education. Basil had been to Winchester and later to Oxford. In sending their boys to public school in Britain, Valerie and Basil were merely observing the traditions of the class from which they came. Nowadays, parents considering the boarding school option might wonder at the distances involved, or query the advisability of having children form school relationships that would not be kept up during the holidays, when neighbourhood pals would once again become the centre of attention. But all of this is mere hindsight. The fact that Basil and Valerie employed a number of servants and sent their children to public school in Britain is not so terribly important in itself, but it does throw some light on their world and its values.

Central to that world was a certain code of personal conduct and restrained emotional behaviour. As Tim saw it: 'You didn't talk about money, sex or your emotions. They did break the taboos a little, but I was never aware of talk about money when I was growing up. My father was not a man who could talk about his innermost emotions. He was embarrassed. But he had a brilliant way with words, so he did express them in an indirect, amusing way. But I never heard him say I love you'. While there seems to be no doubt that Basil did not indulge in verbal expression of his feelings, his letters are ample proof of the fact that he was far from devoid of emotion. Ham is emphatic that his father was not a cold man. 'Neither of them was physically demonstrative – with each other or with us. That was probably a fault. They simply were not capable of public affection and they had this physical restraint. But it is not right to conclude that because of this outward restraint that they were not privately close.' Ham points out that his father did expect his sons to understand his feelings for them. In the *Canyon And I*, which Basil wrote when he was dying, he said: 'I'm sure as a battleship's anchor that my wife, my brother, and the boys know about my deep affections. They also know me, and comprehend what I've said about modes of expression. Actually, come to think of it, I believe they'd incline to the same mode'.

Geraldine Cruess-Callaghan tells a story that provides an insight into Basil's code of behaviour. 'I remember visiting him when he was very ill in St Michael's Hospital. I was in black because my own husband Cedric had died. Cedric had not wanted a big funeral and I carried out his wishes. He had died early in the morning on a Friday. He was buried on the Saturday, but I didn't put it in the papers until the weekend. Basil congratulated me on doing it that way. He felt he didn't like big gushy funerals with all the demonstration etc. You see death and sex were similar for Basil: both were private. Looking back now, I can't ever remember seeing Basil kiss Valerie in public.' Valerie acknowledged this shared reticence in a letter she wrote to Basil while travelling to South Africa with Ham in 1970: 'Do remember Darling, I am not always very articulate but I love you with all my heart and admire your brilliance and versatility. Also you are such a wonderful and gentle lover! I can say quite truthfully I love you more now than when we first married and that was completely.'[7] It is worth bearing in mind that Valerie wrote these lines after thirty-one years of marriage.

With hindsight, it is possible for outsiders to question the impact of all this emotional reticence, the lack of physical demonstrativeness and the boarding school experience, on the three Goulding boys. But in different ways each of them expresses the view that it is wrong to criticise their parents for sending them to public school. It was the well-worn path for children of their class and generation. Tim says that it was only in later life that he began to question the whole experience. 'It was normal to be sent off: a *fait accompli*. But looking back I was a little boy in short trousers put on the mailboat at seven years of age. I woke up in Ludgrove thinking I'm not going to see my Mummy and Daddy for three months, or maybe they'd come over once during the term. But when you're that age and you do something well, like win the hundred yards or do well in Latin, you want to tell your Mummy and Daddy. It's a terribly lonesome experience. I'd never do it to a child of mine. But you kept a stiff upper lip and it wasn't a problem because in those days one wasn't allowed to have a problem. As a forty-eight-year-old looking back, it's hideous. A forcing ground for these repressed upper-class English people who are going to be leaders. I'm sure many of them end up with emotional problems. It was very militaristic and uncaring. But I wouldn't have told my mother then. I had lots of tantrums as a child, and I used to attack my mother. I was very lonely.'

Lingard says he was homesick when he first went off to school in England, but he's not 'in any way critical of my parents for sending me. It was the way children from our situation were brought up'.

God bless nanny, mummy, daddy, Tim, Ham, etc, etc. These, my earliest nocturnal prattlings, show that in those days my mother had to settle for second place in my affections. The time and place was wartime Britain and the anecdote exemplifies one of her outstanding characteristics: her unquestioning response to the call of duty. Although recently married to an Irishman (who acted likewise), she nevertheless volunteered for the army at the outset of war, becoming firstly a 'FANY' (First Aid Nursing Yeomanry), then a sergeant in the 'ATS' and finally receiving a commission as the no. 1 cadet. She left her first-born son in the excellent care of a nanny (who now approaches her century on the Isle of Wight) with whom he floated around England, successfully dodging the bombs and sleeping in metal shelters.

Modern mothers might find this value-judgement difficult to comprehend, but it must be remembered that in 1940 Britain was a very different nation and the War Effort was paramount in the eyes of most of His Majesty's subjects – personal considerations such as self and family had to be subjugated. In another sense it was a thoroughly modern action for a woman to go to war – the women of ancient Sparta, that most bellicose of cities, waited at home to reward their menfolk with their attentions, should they return.

My memories of those early years with my nanny are inevitably hazy, but foremost among them was the pleasant anticipation of my parents' visits. I was certainly a self-centred little boy (as indeed, most children are) and for five whole years I held sway on my own centre court and was a Very Important Person. (Perhaps Freud would attribute my subsequent shortcomings to my mother's absences during those 'formative years', but Freud is dead and I have survived.)[8]

Talking about his relationship with his mother, more than eight years after the above article was published in the *Sunday Tribune*, Lingard says, 'Nanny was number one in my life because I knew her best. In my prayers she came first. She was a surrogate mother. She was a tremendous influence in my life, and even after she left when I was about twelve, I used to go and stay with her for holidays'. Faced with the outbreak of war, Lingard explains that there was no alternative for people like his parents: 'My mother has a strong sense of duty. That's the kind of people they were'. Ham remembers his childhood as being dominated by the awe with which he regarded his parents. 'The central thing in my youth is the reverence and respect that I felt for my parents. There are different ways of loving. I didn't have the closeness that you'd have with parents who were with you every day and who change your nappies and know the problems that you encounter every minute of the day. But it doesn't diminish the way you love them. I think I thought that everyone's family had a clinic, and I never knew what my father did or what went on in the office. I didn't spend my time yearning for her to come home from the clinic, but I did look forward to their coming home and the sound of the car on the gravel. I never felt a lack of love or support from my family. I have no sense of longing for more affection.'

Both Basil and Valerie appeared god-like to their young sons. Tim always uses the term Olympian to describe his father. 'I was in awe of him. He was so busy, an ideas man. I loved him dearly but he didn't suffer fools gladly. If someone talked nonsense he'd stop listening. It wasn't really until much later in life that I began to question why I was remote from him. He wasn't good at relating to small children. Dad would come in from work and either go straight out to talk to the gardeners or else he would go to his study or the drawingroom and work on papers until dinner. After dinner he would often work again. Then in the morning he'd do his Canadian airforce exercises and go out into the garden before going to work. On the weekend he was involved in sports or the garden. We lived in a place that was like Heaven when we were growing up. I often wondered why he never stopped to enjoy it. He was always doing something, like replanting. It's a pity he was never really able to stop until he became ill. In a way he flowered then. He opened up a lot on the emotional level at the end.'

Ham felt overwhelmed as a child. 'I was a very timid person. I was the youngest and felt as if I was surrounded by giants. I was often afraid to open my mouth. My father had such a sharp intellect and knowledge so whatever he said was right and the same with my mother and two brothers. I kept my head down. I was afraid that if I said something it would be ridiculed. Not that it often was, but I felt they were superior to me. I was afraid to try anything in case it wouldn't work. How could you approach a standard like his? This man could make beautiful furniture, play two or three instruments, he was top of all the sports, and intellectually very strong. He could talk philosophy, religion and literature. What do you do? You know you can't win. My solution was to keep the head down.'

According to Lingard, Basil wanted 'to know at the end of the day what we had achieved. He wanted every half-hour to be filled. The answer was often not much. I think my self-esteem went down a bit. Both my parents were great achievers. One feels that one has a lot to live up to. But most children of distinguished parents feel like that. In my teens I was a bit negative. My father would get irritated if I just lay in bed and didn't do anything. He wanted action all of the time. It rubbed up a bit. I became a bit isolated. I still feel guilty now when I'm not active'. On the other hand, Ham doesn't feel that his father demanded a daily record of achievement but he acknowledges that the pressure was there in a subtle way. Tim regards his parents' constant need to achieve as part of a wider pattern of behaviour and conditioning. 'Both of them were driven by the Protestant work ethic. Dad was appalled if any of us were sitting around doing nothing. He couldn't relate to that at all. In my mother's case, I think she had this feeling that she had to measure up. Her father, Walter Monckton, was God to her. There was this constant theme of duty and that one must do something. She had this pressure to achieve and she needed to be one of the boys.'

A person's recollection of events can very often be at odds with another individual's memory, though exactly the same situation was experienced. This is particularly true where emotions are involved. Annie remembers the effect of Basil's need to be active on the household. 'We'd often play cards with our neighbours, the Barringtons, and we'd hear Basil's car coming up the drive. We'd hide everything because you'd have to appear to be doing something. I think there was a lot of the Protestant work ethic there.' At home, Basil's personal behaviour was referred to as O and A – organisation and administration. In this he was in stark contrast to Valerie, who takes little interest in the things around her. The compulsion for order, activity and achievement is perhaps well exemplified in a letter Basil sent to Tim while he was at Winchester. The letter, which is filed amongst a batch of correspondence relating to the boy's education, is, for the outsider at least, acerbic in tone:

> Dear Tim,
>
> It now seems apparent that an orthodox school-university sequence is not for you – or rather you for it.
>
> Your reports are unanimous in showing that you do not (which is not necessarily the same as cannot) offer enough application to hard-work subjects to command them. This is even the case in the subject which suits you, Art; where as soon as some slogging is needed in Art History – progress has to be recorded as Dim.
>
> I do not find attractive, and it is now pretty clearly ineffective as well, paying enormous sums to give you any more Winchester: moreover, lack of

achievement in its curriculum now seems automatically to arrange that a University is not to follow.

Now I am not accusing you of being a No Good. Far from it, because I appreciate and enjoy the many other things you do (than Work) and your zest and versatility in doing them. More power to these. That, in fact, is what I write about.

We propose to take you away from Winchester at the end of this half. I have wired Mr Manisty to this effect — and to get you straightaway involved in the daily, and five-year, work — or more accurately Work — of qualifying as an architect . . . .

I suppose you will be disappointed at missing Cloister Time. But there is little purpose in it, for you are not on the edge of any special attainment (eg Lords). Therefore it would seem practical to get busy as soon as possible to achieve a well-recognised professional status in a field where aesthetics, your forte, play a leading role, but where sheer continued application to the whole structure of a big subject plays one at least as important.[9]

It appears that as with many other aspects of his personal dealings Basil was more comfortable on paper than he was face to face. This coincided with the house rules, which essentially vetoed direct confrontation on any subject. According to Ham, there was never 'any shouting. No raised voices or harsh words. If there was a problem it would be dealt with by a bit of sarcasm or sulking but no overt aggression – except for Tim'. Lingard was only slapped once during his entire childhood. 'I had been rude to my grandmother. He gave me a belt on the backside and this had a huge effect on me. I was in tears for ages though there was no pain in it. It was the only time that he struck me.' Years later, when Basil was dying, Tim, in particular, grew closer to his father. But looking back on his childhood relationship with his parents he feels that his father was very remote. 'In any upset or delicate situation – it was Mum's room that we went to.' The need for parental approval is a common phenomenon, but in a household where children felt somewhat dwarfed in the shadow of, what Ham describes as, 'giants', that need took on an acute edge. Lingard, perhaps more than the others, and because he was the eldest, is open about the need for his parents validation. 'I failed to get into Oxford. That was a bit of a blow to me. A lot of my friends were in England and a lot of the things I loved doing were taking place in England. It was always assumed at home that I would be a businessman even though I had no career guidance or anything. After university I went into lead and zinc mining in Australia. I had an introduction out there and started work the day after I arrived. I had decided during university that I had to go abroad or else I would end up in a nine-to-five job. That was an enriching time for me. I began as a work-study officer, clicking watches at people. Then I got into computers. I was looking for a mathematical model for the mining industry. When I started, we didn't even have a computer at Broken Hill. When I came home I worked for two years in Goulding's. We installed the first third-generation computer in Ireland. Then I was involved with Rionore – making jewellery – which was one of my father's early diversification projects. My job was to administer and sell; I was not particularly good at either role. It failed in the end because it was too labour intensive. But by 1969 I was becoming disenchanted. I knew I wasn't in my niche. I was the boss's son in a big organisation. I wanted to do something on my own. I approached Duncan White who was a friend of mine, looking for advice. He was the assistant headmaster at Brooke House School. He suggested that I join the school for a year. So I retired from Goulding's, went to Trinity and did the Higher Diploma in Education. After about four years at Brooke House I was approached and asked to take over Headfort School. That was in 1977. Sometime in 1979 my parents came down to the school for the weekend. There was a reception and the staff met them and they saw the school in action with me at the helm – that's the way my father would have viewed it. He was happy because I'd made a mark. He sent me a letter afterwards saying how glad he was that I'd found a niche. Prior to that my career had been pretty chequered. That was one happy memory.'

Many things look different in retrospect or hindsight. Tim thinks that there is a tendency to see 'disadvantage in almost any childhood. People would question whether we had the warm closeness that some families have. It is true that Dad was Olympian until we were much older and we didn't see that much of Mum – she was out working. But I didn't feel the lack of home life then. It was only later when I was feeling all these things in my teens and I had nobody to say it to. They were both so busy. Dad was a workaholic. Mum loved the holidays and

Dad hated it, except for the skiing. Our trips to the west of Ireland and Connemara were the best times, when we were all together, camping in an old cowshed by the sea. We used to go to France and bicycle around. Skiing was really great. It was a time when we would all be together as a family, nobody else, no staff. They were magic times. With today's perspective, I would like to have had Mum home more often. But I've never nurtured any wounds that she should have been with me more. Prince Charles probably thinks he was normal in his youth.'

Looking back on life at Dargle, Tim remembers a house full of laughter and funny pranks. 'Dad was always up to something. Typical of the kind of thing that he would do was the time he made a surprise dinner for Mum. He made a salmon mousse and put it into two half-globe shapes on the table. Then he put a bra on top with two cherries on either side. I'm not so sure what Mum thought of that.' Artist Bobby Ballagh remembers afternoon tea being taken in the most exquisite china while 'the boys' played indoor cricket. On raising his cup of Earl Grey the artist remembers finding an egg bobbing on the surface.

Valerie became a Roman Catholic in 1962. She was led through her conversion process by Archdeacon McCarthy, who was then president of Clonliffe College. By all accounts, the archdeacon spent as much time helping Basil through Valerie's transformation as he did helping the applicant herself. How Basil reacted to this major change in his wife's life is a somewhat disputed issue, with various friends, family and Valerie, expressing conflicting views. Valerie is sometimes inclined to understate the unpalatable: a device she appears to have used when it came to dealing with the differences between herself and Basil over religion. 'I don't think he believed in God. He was a twice-a-year man. I didn't talk to him about religion much, but I didn't worry about his faith because I was so sure of how good he was. I knew he would be in Heaven before me. He lived a good life. It was only when I became a Catholic that we discussed it with the archdeacon. They exchanged many letters. I think he was a bit horrified when I said I was changing. I think he thought that I'd be different. I told him that it would make no difference to our lives and that I wouldn't talk about it. He had this idea that if I became a Catholic that I'd rush around with a placard screaming "I'm a Roman Catholic". I think he feared that I'd become garrulous and become a converter. If I hadn't married Basil I would have become a Catholic when my brother Gilbert changed. We were so close to it in any case, with Papa being an Anglo-Catholic for most of his life. But in Ireland I saw the difficulties, and I couldn't just get married and then say that I was changing. I waited nearly twenty-five years, but the wish was always there and I talked to my brother about it a lot. I knew that I always wanted to be a Catholic. I just felt nearer to God in a Catholic church. I felt He was there. I didn't have that feeling in a Protestant church.'

Valerie did not regard the different moral and social teachings of the Catholic church as a potential difficulty in her marriage. 'No, that was easy, thanks to the archdeacon. He told Basil that as a Protestant he could do what he liked. I ignored the bits about contraception and the archdeacon more or less told Basil that I should go by my husband's wishes. The social aspects of the teaching didn't come into it for me. None of my children had an interest in religion, and therefore when divorce became a family issue there was no religion involved.' Ham feels that it is difficult to unravel the complexity of the feelings and emotions that transpired between his parents when Valerie converted. Much of it, he feels, was left unsaid. 'I don't know what was going on and how it worked. I don't know how either of them tolerated each other's views. I don't believe that the concept of her making the move was a problem. But the day-to-day manifestations must have caused a problem. Like the fact that she wanted to go to Mass when he wanted to do something else. It would have been different if he had been committed to another religion. His view was that the whole thing was rubbish. That must have hurt her and perhaps that was insensitive. He would come out with desperate condemnations like "Jesus Mary and Joseph – that's what you say when you burn the toast". I think that there was a lot of disagreement hidden there. I don't understand why she converted. I think that my father's vitriolic attacks on religion must have been damaging for her, and the way she pursued the thing must have been irksome to him.'

Tim sees the religious issue as one of the areas where his mother and father did not understand each other. 'I think that there was tolerance there and that's why they didn't talk about it that much. I think that my father felt that if religion was what Valerie wanted, then he should leave her to it. He thought it was mumbo-jumbo. I don't think he respected it at all, because he was a man of rigorous intellectual principle, and he couldn't square Catholicism with that. There are many inconsistencies in my mother's religious beliefs. It's emotional, not intellectual. She goes for the feeling.' One of Basil's close friends feels that Valerie's conversion was the only time that he saw any great tension between them. 'He was hurt by it. He told me that it hurt him a lot. He said that it was hard to be as close to somebody who had changed their religion and was no longer the same religion as you. I asked him if it really mattered and he got upset. He said that it meant choosing a different road and that one could never be that close again. I felt he was unhappy during that time. But there wasn't much one could do. The archdeacon was there many a weekend. Basil seemed to get on with him.'[10]

Lingard disagrees with the view of the conversion expressed by his father's friend. 'My father was a liberal so it wasn't a problem. He used to pull Fr McCarthy's leg a lot and they exchanged many letters. I went to the ceremony when she was admitted into the Catholic church. I never shared her wish but I don't believe it bothered my father. He did write about religion – *The 99 Articles*. I think it would have given offence if it had been published. It's good that it wasn't. An example of the kind of thing he felt, was his reference to the Catholic view on contraception as "indiscriminate rabbitry".' Brian and Brenda Clarke live very near Dargle Cottage. Basil and Valerie were regulars at the tennis parties they held most Sundays. Since Basil's death the couple have been loyal companions to Valerie. Brian says that 'Basil was shocked when she converted to Roman Catholicism. He took it very badly – I know for certain it was a shock to him'. Brenda points out that Valerie converted at a time when people 'were not going to each other's churches. In changing, she was crossing a chasm. It was a shock. You think you know someone very well and suddenly there's this very powerful influence. He would have realised that he didn't know his wife. The Gouldings had been Protestant for generations. Nowadays one would hardly notice such a thing.'

There is some irony in the fact that it was Valerie's mother and not her beloved father who made a deathbed conversion to Catholicism.

Though Walter had pondered his faith deeply over the years, his personal life as well as other factors prevented him taking the step he had long contemplated. As we have seen, religion, sex and marriage are all intertwined in the story of Valerie's family, and in the period after her own conversion these issues would once again come to the fore when she faced the impending deaths of both her mother and father. Walter and Polly had lived separately from the late 1930s on, but appeared together briefly as man and wife on occasions such as Gilbert's safe return from Dunkirk. As the years wore on, and with their two children married, there was little left to draw them together. For her part, Polly was building a new life, perhaps energised by her experiences as an ambulance driver during the war, while Walter was spending a lot of time travelling to and from India in the course of his work for the Nizam of Hyderabad.

It was there in 1946 that he met Bridget, Countess of Carlisle, known to her friends as Biddy. Valerie tells a story about their meeting which is not repeated in either of the Monckton biographies. 'My father's personal assistant came back from India and when I met him he said to me, "There's something I've got to tell you. I met a lady out there who told me that, though she had never met Walter Monckton, she was determined to marry him. She told me that she had seen him but hadn't talked to him". At that stage she was married to Lord Carlisle and she was head of the ATS out there.' It is safe to presume from the way Valerie tells the story that she was not an admirer of the woman who was to become the second Lady Monckton. According to Lord Birkenhead, Walter met Biddy in Delhi in May and told her straight away that he wanted to marry her, despite the fact that neither of them were then divorced from their previous partners: 'The depth of Walter's love appears in every line of his letters to Lady Carlisle at this time, and it is obvious that he realised that at last he had found fulfilment, and that in contrast to this abiding passion, the other women in his life since the collapse of his marriage, were the creatures of an hour.'[11]

In the summer of 1947, as Valerie waited for Ham to be born and Walter waited for his divorce to come through, she wrote to him telling him not to worry about money:

I did have a word with him [Gilbert] on the phone, and he then said something about a will but I didn't gather what, but don't worry about it. Why should you, and don't go sweating to earn money to leave behind. All I think is necessary is that Mummy should have a fair amount to live on, anyhow this is all very morbid and a long way off, but please don't let it worry you.[12]

Valerie did not stay with Walter and Biddy when she visited England. She says that her father knew her feelings though the issue was never discussed. 'She was cute enough. She knew how close my father and I were so she went out of her way to be nice to me.' Gilbert shares Valerie's view of their stepmother. 'The second marriage was a disaster from our point of view. Valerie and I were left four thousand pounds each from a man who was once a millionaire. I think he was bewitched by her. Perhaps it was a sexual thing like the Duke and Duchess of Windsor. But he wasn't happy near the end, when he was ill and dying. The doctor wrote to me and told me to get Walter away. My wife Marianna tried to help, but Biddy wouldn't have it.'

Walter and Polly became seriously ill at about the same time. It was a very difficult period for Valerie, who spent much of 1964 travelling to and from England to be with her mother in London and her father in Sussex. Polly had been diagnosed as having liver cancer at the end of 1963, while Walter began to display the symptoms that we now associate with Alzheimer's disease.

My Darling Lingard,

What will you be thinking of me, no letters for such a long time. I really couldn't bring myself to write I have been so upset by poor Marzi [Polly]. I have been to and fro from London trying to get nurses and at times having to give her injections. She is still alive but I think it will only be a day or two now. However, at long last the doctor seems to have got something that stops the pain. A fortnight ago Grandpa nearly died, he was in Iraq and got a stroke, however he recovered from this, but last week got a bad virus infection. Yesterday I heard that he was out of danger and I hope will be coming home in about a fortnight. On top of it all I got a duodenal ulcer which started to bleed, but I have been in bed for the past week and am now getting better rapidly.[13]

When Polly was ill and knew that she was dying, she asked both Gilbert and Valerie to tell Walter that she forgave him. Valerie says she was able to give her father her mother's message, but Gilbert wasn't sure if Walter received the information he tried to pass on. 'My mother wrote to me and told me to tell him that she'd forgiven him, but I couldn't get through to him because he was so ill. I put it in writing but I'm not sure if Biddy passed it on.' Reflecting on his mother's deathbed act of forgiveness, Gilbert feels that Polly 'would have tolerated his indiscretions had they been discreet – but they weren't'. According to both Valerie and Gilbert, Biddy was not anxious to have either of them with Walter during his illness, despite the fact that she was having difficulty nursing him. 'When he was dying Biddy resented me going to see him. She allowed me to stay for two weeks so that she could get away. But she didn't want any of his friends to stay. The doctor told me that he didn't know what kind of reception I'd get when I arrived as Biddy was constantly telling him that he didn't want to see me. I think she thought that we'd talk Catholicism to him.'

A report written by Dr Anthony Churcher, Walter's GP, appears to support Gilbert and Valerie's concern for their father. The report begins by stating that Walter was suffering from dementia and that his condition had caused a state of dependence on objects old and familiar.

> Lady Monckton has found it very difficult to manage him. She tries to imagine that he is still a fit man. She finds it impossible to devote her full attention to his wellbeing. She has admitted in the past that 'I am the worst possible person for Walter'. When Lady Monckton upsets her husband this is liable to aggravate his confusion and produce acute agitation. Lady Monckton has seen numerous famous consultants about her husband and all have told her that it is a question of management not drugs. She has realised this but her management has only slightly improved. She is so anxious and apprehensive that at times she is unable to manage him whilst a firm but kind nurse manages the patient. Lady Monckton has been advised to spend part of the week in town and the week-end as Lord Monckton's wife with his Lordship in the country. This she utterly refuses to do despite agreeing to the suggestion on the phone.
>
> Although Lord Monckton is at times confused he does have lucid periods. It is during these lucid periods that he has told his children, nurses, medical attendants and even Lady Monckton his wish to go and live with his children. He has told me about five times on different occasions. He feels at times that

if he took his life Biddy would be free but when asked how he would – replied that 'a friend would lend him a gun' and on another occasion that 'I will fall to the ground'. This phase rapidly passes into one of leaving Lady Monckton on the grounds that if she is unable to devote all her time to him then she might if he threatened to go.

There are two solutions to this very difficult problem.

1. Lady Monckton takes the advice of her numerous medical advisers. If she spent most of the week away and the week-end in constant attendance. This she is most unlikely to do.

2. Lord Monckton goes to live with his children accompanied by a nurse. This at first may produce confusion and a desire to return to his wife. However within 48 hours he will feel and be less confused.

The only person who can make the decision to go is Lord Monckton and there are times when he is fully aware of the consequences of such a decision. There is no doubt in my mind that it is much easier to handle him when Lady Monckton is away and this has been confirmed by all the nurses he has had in the past six months.[14]

Two months before his death, Walter left his house near Folkington in Sussex and was married to Biddy in a church ceremony conducted by his friend Bishop Mervyn Stockwood. Both Polly and Lord Carlisle were now dead and he was free to seek the proper marriage service he wanted. On 6 January 1965 both Valerie and Gilbert were present when Walter received Communion. He died three days later. There is bitterness in Valerie's recollection of the church service. 'The padre asked us if Gilbert and I would like to say some of the prayers at the service even though we were Catholic but Biddy refused to allow this. We arranged a cross with poppies on it but she didn't want our flowers on the coffin. Just her own.' Though Walter had moved away from Anglo-Catholicism under the guidance of Mervyn Stockwood, who had helped him through the spiritual ostracism he felt after his divorce, he expressed satisfaction on hearing of Valerie's conversion. Earlier, when Gilbert became a Catholic at Cambridge, he told his son that he was delighted for him. But Stockwood kept Walter in the Anglican fold as a 'good middle-of-the-road churchman'.[15] And so it was Polly who, in the end, concluded the spiritual journey she had first begun with Walter when they exchanged letters from the Front.

Gilbert was a friend of Monseigneur Alfred Gilbey, a Catholic priest.

'I hadn't rung him when my mother was dying. But then there was a knock on the door and I went out and there was Monseigneur Gilbey. My mother said "Thank God". She was received there and then. We had a Requiem Mass two days later in St Mary's Church, Cadogan Street, where I had been married to Marianna and where all my children were christened.'

> My Darling Lingard,
>
> Thank you for your very sweet letter. Marzi died on the 30th [April, 1964] and really after the way she had suffered one could only have wished it for her. For the past fortnight I was with her she was without pain, then the last few days it came back, the doctor was marvellous and did what he could and eventually she went into a coma before the end. We have had some wonderful letters about her, but yours was one of the best.[16]

It is obvious from any perusal of Walter Monckton's papers and from any conversation with both Valerie and Gilbert, that religion was a source of both angst and solace for their father. Later Valerie's own conversion drew a mixed reaction from her family and their friends. Because Valerie enjoyed a public role in Ireland, especially during the 1960s and 1970s, she was open to cynical gossip about the motivation for her conversion. There were those who whispered that it too was part of her public relations exercises. That view is hard to square with the sheer weight of the evidence of the importance of religion in her father's life. And Valerie, even as a middle-aged woman, was very much her father's daughter.

---

1 Russell Murphy was a well-known Dublin accountant. Following his death it was alleged that he had embezzled funds from his clients' accounts.

2 Basil to Valerie while she was in England.

3 Basil writing to Valerie from London during his recuperation after his back operation on 26 February 1947. 'Wog' was a pet name for Basil; 'Sall' was a pet name for the baby Valerie was expecting (their third child, Ham).

4 Valerie's eldest son Lingard is the headmaster at Headfort School and is not married. Tim is separated from his wife Annie and has a daughter, Camille. He works in a studio at his home in Allihies in West Cork. Ham is separated from his wife Vonnie and has two children, Barnes and Lia. He is a pilot with Aer Lingus and lives near his mother in Wicklow.

5 A business friend of Basil's in an interview with the author.

6 Basil to Valerie, 27 October 1954.

7 An undated letter at the Army and Navy Club in London, which Ham says was written in 1970.

8 Lingard Goulding writing in the *Kindred* column in the *Sunday Tribune*, 22 September 1985.

9 Basil to Tim at Winchester, 25 January 1963.

10 A close friend of Basil's in conversation with the biographer.

11 *Walter Monckton – The Life of Viscount Monckton of Brenchley*. Lord Birkenhead. Weidenfeld and Nicholson, London 1969, p223.

12 Dep. Monckton Trustees 41. F, 9, 11–12–17, 28, 89–90. Valerie to Walter, 7 June 1947.

13 Valerie to Lingard in Australia, 12 April 1964.

14 Undated memo on Dr Anthony Churcher's notepaper in Lady Goulding's possession. This is a carbon-copy of the original document.

15 *Walter Monckton – The Life of Viscount Monckton of Brenchley*. Lord Birkenhead. Weidenfeld and Nicholson, London 1969, p273.

16 Valerie to Lingard in Australia, 7 May 1964.

7

WILLIE B

Basil was a grand actor in his own life. For him life was a great stage and he wanted to play a lot of roles. Inelegance was unforgivable: he was not a snob in the social sense but a snob in the way you did things. Style was everything for Basil.

Basil Goulding would not have disagreed with Dr Tony O'Reilly's assessment of him. Talking to Henry Kelly in the *The Irish Times* around the time of his retirement, Basil described the background from which he came:

> I went from Winchester straight to Oxford. Not to have done so would have been looked upon as very improper. It was the automatic progression. I didn't really go to Oxford actually, like everyone else at school, I meandered there. One's parents in those days didn't give one an educational menu and suggest you pick a dish. You just went and were expected to do everything with an easy grace, with an easy elegance. You see, the difference between my university days and now is that in my day you were expected to be the perfect amateur: you had to shine at sport but you were never to be seen practising, and at the same time you were expected to get a good second-class degree but never to be caught studying or anything like that. Nowadays you have what I call the three great Ws: permanent work, a permanent woman and, as a consequence, permanent worry.[1]

After Basil died in January 1982, Dr O'Reilly wrote *The Irish Times* obituary:

> 'B' IS FOR Basil (or Willie B, as Valerie lovingly called him); it is also for – Brave; and – Benign; and – Byronic; and all those things that described a man of valour and unique accomplishment in a world of increased uniformity. He was a man who enchanted those fortunate to be his friends with the

originality of his mind, the gentleness of his ways and the constant pitch of his humour.

Who else but Basil would have attended a vital Bank of Ireland board meeting on skates or worn a gigantic frog on the lapels of his evening jacket as he appeared for a formal dinner party? It was a measure of the man that with his stern good looks and magnificent carriage, nobody dared ask was the frog a friend or merely someone along for the ride. I can still see him fixing the waiter with an unblinking eye and saying: 'I'll have a gin and tonic and my friend takes Perrier water!'.

Evelyn Waugh's 'Brideshead Revisited' has cast us back to the elegance of the Thirties and there was much of that elegance about Basil Goulding; a certain grace of movement, a gift of epigram, a sort of dedicated amateurism that infused all his actions with a degree of chivalry and gallantry.

His business style was to the uninitiated often prolix and yet, having read and re-read his famous 'Chairman's Bones' for Fitzwilton, I am amazed at the clarity of his mind and the simplicity with which he stated basic business principles. He would have been a dazzling university professor with a spirit younger than the student body and a capacity to articulate his knowledge in a contemporary way.

His appetite for life was enormous and captured only in part by his accomplishments. Sportsman extraordinary in soccer, cricket, tennis, squash and skiing.

An art collector of discernment and yet catholic taste, a gardener in the mould of 'Capability' Brown – part architect – part agronomist – he was a man whose talents and curiosity exceeded by a sum the passage of a single day or, sadly, the span of a single lifetime.

As he lay dying a week ago, lying in his bed and looking out at his beloved Dargle Glen, he had no bitterness, no recrimination, no anger at the imminence of the unknown – just curiosity and a sort of impatience at tasks undone and plans uncompleted. Though greatly weakened by his illness, he pored over architects' drawings of a new development on his property and reviewed with me the draft of a book that surveys the nature of his condition and the implication of his death. Need I say that the draft revealed the same clear eye and original humour that had characterised his observation on life in our times.

His epitaph is a simple one. He hugely enjoyed his life, he enriched the lives of his friends, he contributed to the quality of life in his community and his country, he assisted his great and charitable wife in her Christian endeavours. He left the world a better place for his children – oh that we could all enjoy such a commendation.[2]

In his generous obituary Dr O'Reilly draws on most of Basil's many and varied interests in life, though as obituaries tend to do, he passes quickly over his business abilities, which received more critical comment than his undoubted excellence as a sportsman, gardener and connoisseur of art. The bare facts of Basil's business life are that he took over the chairmanship of W & H M Goulding Ltd when his father died in 1935; in the summer of 1972 the Goulding companies were involved in a reverse takeover by Fitzwilliam Securities, a shell company headed by Tony O'Reilly, Vincent Ferguson and Nicholas Leonard; following the installation of a Bank of Ireland representative on the board of the new Fitzwilton Ltd, Basil retired as chairman in 1976. After the reverse takeover the name Goulding went, as did the company's primary activity, the manufacture and supply of fertiliser. There is, of course, behind these bare facts, the bigger human story of the many jobs that were lost and the lives that were changed by the collapse of what had been one of the country's most solid companies. There is too the other story of what Basil was trying to do when he invited the young and acquisitive O'Reilly to join forces with his staid and predominantly Protestant firm. And when it was all over, how did Basil feel about the loss of the Goulding dynasty and what, if any, was the effect on Valerie?

W & H M Goulding stands for William and Humphreys Manders Goulding who started an agricultural supplies company in the 1840s. According to family legend, Humphreys Manders discovered fertiliser when he accidentally dropped acid onto bone, which dissolved and then dropped onto a plant. In 1872 the firm became a Limited Company and according to the prospectus it had five hundred appointed agents in the United Kingdom, France, Portugal, Russia and America. It was also noted in the prospectus that Goulding's was the first firm to ship a cargo of manure into the United States, and was exporting to Natal and Norway.[3] The firm relied on phosphate of one kind or another and so an essential part of its business was securing enough of its base manufacturing component. By the 1890s the company, with its two main bases in Dublin and Cork, was in a position to buy a controlling interest in Richardson's Chemical Manure Company in Derry. In 1902 a new factory was built in Waterford, leaving Goulding's in a strong position to distribute its product with its six factories in Derry, Belfast, Dublin, Waterford and Cork.

From 1920 to the commencement of the Second World War, production of fertilisers showed a steady increase from the eight factories in operation and the total deliveries rose to 178,000 tons. The death occurred in 1925 of Sir William Joshua Goulding who was created a Baronet in 1904, and the Chairmanship of the Company was taken over by his son, Sir Lingard Amphlett Goulding, who held this office until his death in 1935, when the post was taken over by the present Chairman, Sir Basil Goulding.[4]

Not only was the ownership of Goulding's a dynasty, so was its management. Joseph Milne, a native of Aberdeen, joined the company in 1877 and became general manager in 1894. In turn his son William Milne joined the company in 1899 and when Joseph retired in 1930 he too became general manager. When Basil reluctantly took the helm in 1935 there was another Milne, Billy, waiting in the wings to continue the business connection of these two Protestant families.

Basil had not relished the prospect of joining the family firm but, as we saw earlier, he was dissuaded by both family and circumstance from pursuing his natural inclination, which was architecture. Things got off to a bad start for Basil when he ran into a history professor on his first day at Oxford: 'It meant I studied history, a subject in which I had no interest then and to which I have a positive revulsion now. All history teaches is how to apply totally outdated methods and means to quite changed circumstances'.[5] Whatever about his unusual views on the study of history, Basil's 'meandering' at Oxford did not prepare him for either the fertiliser business or any other kind of business. After Oxford, he set about attempting to rectify this lacuna by studying both the rudiments of science and by taking a business studies course in London. As Valerie sees it, 'Basil wasn't pleased by having to go into the family business. I didn't know him when he actually went in but I know it wasn't his thing. He was a man who loved paintings and gardens and ideas, but he wasn't really a businessman. I don't know how he kept it going for so long. When his father died I think he wasn't able to tell his mother that he wanted to do something else'.

Michael Walker joined the Cork branch of Goulding's in 1966 as an agronomist and sales representative. He points out that 'it was every agricultural student's dream to get a job in the company. It was seen as a job for life. It was pensionable at the end and enjoyable in the middle. It was a patriarchal company and run almost for the employees, by a benevolent board of employers and directors who gave the appearance of caring for each worker. If you did right by them then they did right by you. And in the early days when I joined there was no reason to suspect that there was a problem. One felt that few of the Goulding people were management-trained. The social thing was very important. The impression I had was that if you had been to the right school and played a good game of tennis then you were in'. Neither Basil nor Billy Milne were members of the Masonic Order, though according to Michael Walker, who is now involved in the administration of the Order in Dublin, 'a lot of people in Goulding's were. The Masonic thing wasn't a factor though, certainly by the time I was there'.

Heather Welsh, who was Basil's secretary from 1954 until his retirement in 1976, describes it as a 'family type of company. I remember one day it was foggy in Dublin and the word came down from Billy Milne that the ladies were to be allowed to go home early to make sure that they caught their buses. You felt you had a job for life. The men had their pension scheme, though the women didn't when I started. There was a canteen that was subsidised by the company, but that all changed after 1972. Basil wasn't a Mason or anything like that, but it was very much a Protestant company in the 1950s. When I came over from Scotland I was determined to make friends from outside Goulding's as well as inside, otherwise I would have only met a certain section of people'.

Billy Milne was joint managing director with J W Parkes, and joined the company in 1937. 'I knew Basil from the early 1930s. My grandfather came to Goulding's in 1877, then my father succeeded him and then it was me. Basil was dumped into the chairmanship very early on because of the tragic death of his father in 1935. He knew nothing about business and my father carried him. Lord Wargrave, the Rolls Royce man, was very friendly with my father, and as Basil's uncle he had asked my father to look after Basil. My father took Basil under his wing, but he never took a great interest in the business. After the war there was the question of what Basil was to do. By then my father was an old man. I felt Basil was under pressure then to go to London – they did have good connections there. My father agreed that someone with a title based in London would be better leading the company. It was a kind of a game that my father played, that Basil was the frontman. In my time it worked that way as well – I was happy to let it go that way. Basil was primarily an ideas man. He was absolutely brilliant. He would come in and dump an idea on my desk and ask me what I thought. I couldn't say that's a lot of nonsense: I'd have to satisfy him that it was a lot of nonsense: nine times out of ten it was rubbish or something out of context, but if there was something in it he'd expect you to drop everything and work the idea out for him. Then he'd be like a terrier with a rabbit. Anything that he took up he went all out at it.'

During the 1960s Basil began to look out for ways of diversifying the firm's interests, and so Goulding's became involved in sack and bag manufacture, office construction, jewellery-making, portable huts, straw-based building components, pianos and even a proposal to build a tennis court. Looking back, perhaps with the somewhat jaundiced eye of someone who lost his job after the Fitzwilton deal, Michael Walker describes the diversifications as 'sidestream ventures started by certain members of the board for their own amusement. There were agronomists who were transferred to the piano outlet. People were sidestepped into completely inappropriate activities. It was utterly ludicrous'. With less passion, Dr O'Reilly says that 'Basil saw the finite limitations of the fertiliser business and he tried to diversify into pianos and into jewellery. It was not a good diversification. Piano-playing, jewellery and tennis courts was a lot of nonsense. When I came in they were some of the first things that we sold'. Apart from being the company's financial controller, Jack Good was also a close friend of Basil's, shared his interest in art, and lived very near the Gouldings in Enniskerry. Jack agreed with many of Basil's diversification ideas and supported his attempts to bring fresh ideas into circulation within the firm. 'Basil had a great idea of having people who were at the top of their jobs to lunch. We told them that it was non-political and non-business. We had the head of the army, customs, revenue and other business people. We started all of that, even before Fitzwilton. We met

Tony O'Reilly in a private room in the Hibernian when he was still at Kerrygold.'

Basil was a man on the look-out for ideas and strategies knowing, but perhaps not realising enough, that the heyday of the fertiliser business was nearing an end. Jim McCarthy, a close friend of Dr O'Reilly and a key figure in the birth of Fitzwilton, points out that by the time Basil began looking for a rich partner to join forces with, fertiliser manufacture was already a shrinking business. 'He anticipated that if Goulding's didn't diversify it was finished. When Goulding's was great it was a monopoly, but the government started NET and then they grant-aided Dutch Shell BP to start Albatross. In effect the government ground down the market percentage. He no longer had 80 per cent of the market.' Derek Hill, who was the group marketing director from 1964, says that the company was convinced that fertiliser was being 'dumped' in Ireland, though they were never able to prove it. Hill argues that there were a number of reasons why Basil was looking outside the firm for talent. 'Gouldings was seen as West-Brit in government circles and I think Basil saw that we needed a new man, a chief executive who would be acceptable and well known here. Con Smith fitted the bill.'

Con Smith had built his business empire around cars. He headed the Smith Group, which had the Renault franchise and was then one of the biggest consortiums in the country. Dr O'Reilly describes him as 'one of the new Elizabethans, valiant, bright, successful and aggressive'. Jack Good remembers Con Smith stopping him on Merrion Row, sometime early in 1972, and suggesting to him that the two businesses should merge. Jack thought the idea a bit wild at the time, but Con came back and the two agreed to set up a meeting. Following lengthy negotiations a merger deal was agreed which would have seen the setting up of a new eighteen-member combined board, with Con Smith as executive vice-chairman and Basil as chairman. The mutual attraction was simple: Goulding's was 'asset rich' and 'earnings thin' while the Smith Group was making good profits but had no assets. After the announcement, Goulding's shares rose fourteen pence and Smith's rose five pence. Valerie remembers how excited Basil was by the project. 'Then I came back one day and he was in bits. Con had been killed in that awful air-crash.' On 18 June 1972 a British European Airways Trident with over a hundred passengers on board fell out of the sky over Staines. Con died, along with eleven members of a delegation from the Confederation of Irish Industry who were travelling to Brussels.

Following the crash, Smith's shares dropped seventeen pence, while Goulding's dropped the fourteen pence they had risen after the merger announcement: but Valerie had an idea, and her idea was the young man she'd first picked out as a potential fundraiser and publicity promoter for the clinic – Tony O'Reilly. The subsequent history of the reverse takeover of Goulding's by O'Reilly's Fitzwilliam Securities is controversial. As far as Valerie is concerned, Tony saved Goulding's. That view is not shared by those who lost their jobs in the asset sales and redundancies that followed. Many of those who suffered cannot understand why Dr O'Reilly is a hero in Valerie's eyes. According to O'Reilly 'the worst decision' he ever made was to meet Basil after the Staines crash. 'It was born of tragedy. My father rang me in West Virginia, at White Sulphur Springs, after he heard that a new company was being formed from the Smith Group and W & H M Goulding. My father was aware that I knew about Goulding's from the time when I was in the Sugar Company. He rang me to tell me about the crash and that Con Smith had been killed. Then Basil rang and asked if we'd consider being the Con Smith to Goulding's that Con had planned to be.

'The following Saturday I drove to Dargle for the first time and I met Basil, Jack Good, Robert Mallard, Tom Murray and some lesser lights. We agreed on the same strategy that Con had planned. I got sucked into the Con Smith philosophy. We went ahead with a reverse takeover of control of Goulding's. We had 54 per cent of a company called Crowe Wilson and we put the two together, which meant that we had 34 per cent of the enlarged company. The fertiliser business looked great in 1972, but by 1975 people were gleefully tearing up fertiliser contracts all over the world and we were left with a raw material, base product, superphosphate, which went from fourteen dollars per ton to sixty-six dollars – we were left with farmers who wouldn't buy the product.' In his Henry Kelly interview, following his forced retirement from Fitzwilton, Basil agreed with O'Reilly's analysis of the turn of events:

> I think there has been a very sharp discovery of the difference between expectation and reality. The reality is that much of what has happened has been outside our control. First of all, the Arab world put up the price of phosphates by more than five times, from fourteen dollars to seventy-five in one year. Energy costs went up, and oil and fuel costs went up. When this happened, the product price went up and the buyers rebelled, the export market collapsed and in all those you have the reason why factories closed.[6]

Tom Murray handled the fertiliser end of the new Fitzwilton company. 'I was the blue-eyed boy in the beginning because the fertiliser end of things was still bringing in over a million a year, though the balance sheets didn't show it. The first thing O'Reilly did when he came in was to have Goulding's assets revalued. That allowed him to borrow to buy all the other things he wanted. But it was on the back of Goulding's, and nobody in '72 and '73 foresaw what was going to happen to the fertiliser business. By the time the banks came in I think the company owed twenty-two million pounds.' Dr O'Reilly claims that the Bank of Ireland 'behaved shamefully' in its dealings with Fitzwilton. 'They dismissed Basil from the board, and put in Michael Dargan, who had no impact. As deputy chairman I decided we would take our basic business and our level of debt – that was the only control the bank had on us – and we would pay down the debt and recover control of our business. It was with a considerable sense of triumph that I accepted Michael Dargan's resignation two years later in 1977. We celebrated, Fitzwilton was redeemed.'

Vincent Ferguson, O'Reilly's partner, says that the banks used Basil as a 'fallguy'. 'In reality, Goulding's would have shut their doors completely without Fitzwilton. It was the fertiliser end of things that went wrong. The 500 per cent increase in the price of rock phosphate nearly dragged the whole company down. It was unfortunate that it happened to us so quickly. The Six Day War was the start of it. In the end we sold our better businesses to pay the banks off. We sold the Coca Cola franchise. The banks used Basil as a fallguy as they didn't dare take on O'Reilly because he controlled Independent Newspapers.

Basil's head was the one that had to roll. The banks were running scared because confidence was at an all-time low. There had been property collapses in the UK. There was a lot of fear around.

'Where I fault them is that when it was clear that the fertiliser business was collapsing, when we went from a profit of four million to a loss of four million, they should have told us to reduce our borrowings by fifteen million over a six-month period. We had large borrowings but we had good assets. If the banks had done it that way we could have realised our assets in an orderly way. It could have been done without the trauma of firing the chairman and putting in their own man. We were selling our assets in a buyer's market. They used the fact that Basil played the buffoon in public as an excuse because they wouldn't take on O'Reilly. In the end we sold the assets for forty million and recapitalised the company and threw the banks off the board. It took two years but Fitzwilton was redeemed.'

Valerie and all her sons agree that Basil did not blame Dr O'Reilly for what happened to Goulding's. His close friend, Jack Good, also agrees. 'Basil didn't feel let down by Tony. I never got any sense of it. I think that we were all let down by the Bank of Ireland. Basil was depressed after it but we all were.' Derek Hill takes the view that the deal as it subsequently worked out was not the one he thought was being done during the O'Reilly/Goulding negotiations at Dargle. Jim McCarthy, O'Reilly's loyal friend, admits that 'Basil might have thought that he was bringing Tony in to be his operator' rather than the takeover it turned out to be. 'Maybe Basil did think Tony was coming into Goulding's in a different context. But I think that he should have started doing something earlier than he did. Then Goulding's could have diversified without Fitzwilton. Basil was probably the wrong face for Gouldings. What he needed was a strong cookie, a tough son of a bitch to do the business for him. Basil needed a minder. The banks hated him because they hate any kind of brilliant person. He was treated as if he was a joke. They thought he was off the wall. Investors thought that Basil's antics were crazy.'

From the perspective of a man like Michael Walker, who lost his job when the banks moved in, O'Reilly's arrival was not a great success. Unlike Valerie, he doesn't regard O'Reilly as Goulding's saviour.

'O'Reilly and the boys were in a different league from the Goulding team. They weren't dilettantes. Goulding's thought they were taking in these boys – they were looking for management skills but these boys had taken over. Goulding's didn't realise what was happening. I think Basil had his eye wiped. They took over the board. We knew that O'Reilly, Ferguson and Leonard were in it for what was in it for them. If they could sell it up and make a penny profit they were happy, and that's what worried us. They had no interest in the business. They might as well have been selling chalk – just as long as they turned this acquisition into added value. We knew that as soon as they could sell us at a profit they would.' A senior Goulding manager agrees that 'the day Tony came in, Basil was no longer in an executive position. He stayed as chairman but he was no longer at the helm. When the bank came in Basil was unhappy to step aside, but that wasn't Tony's doing and Tony was loyal to him'.

Basil never claimed to be a great businessman, but he did chair a large company for over forty years. His style was always controversial in business circles, but really only became a problem after the establishment of Fitzwilton, when a family concern became something quite different. In his curriculum vitae Basil always mentioned his interest in writing: his annual report, the *Chairman's Bones*, was regarded by some as sheer genius and by others as the confused ramblings of a madman. Basil was so convinced that his style of report was far superior to the normal ones, he prepared a book called *My Sainted Grammar – a sort of textbook for a sort of writing*, in which he compared the usual company statement with his favoured style. Included in this unpublished text are two versions of a report for the year ending 1972: the year Con Smith died and Goulding's became Fitzwilton.

> There was nothing unusual about last year that a strike, a calamity, a merger or two didn't account for.
>
> Of these the one that was in seconds overpast, the calamity, lives the most ineliminably in mind. With Con Smith there flew away the experience of frank affections and the prospect of bright adventure.
>
> Thence to speak next of a working dispute resolved or of corporate identity translated were brusque. I would, rather, refer first to changes in the Board.

Mr . . . and Mr . . . resigned in July, what time Imperial Chemical Industries Ltd sold the shareholding of some 20% in Goulding which it had assumed in 1964.

The conjunction of events had relationship, but not, I can resound, of any dire ring. For both colleagues took home their abilities, so broad and troy, in amiable pack – as, thanking them for their course, do we.

Backstage, one can observe that Goulding's latterday excursions into diverse activities had had the consequence that ICI were becoming less and less insumed to fertiliser production and marketing – what had been their pilot purpose in joining us.

So I am glad to notice that though our business divagations did not suit their compass it was yet just these that provided them a golden handshake when they wanted out. One cannot always gybe to such advantage.

Akimbo now, shareholders may reflect that our unaffected association in the N.I. fertiliser firms, which prosper under ICI control, is still of great – this year greater – annual comfort to us. The consonant key in which that association plays allows that whatever opportunities arise for economic advancement – perhaps ahead of political – between North and South have easier potential for us than for 'most any . . . .

But now I have almost broached the great merger magnum, and must be thinking how best for you to taste it. My prospect fixes on three shifts.

First, the year past was run to its tape by events of the Goulding firm alone. So I shall run along of them for you.

Second, I can immodestly accept, if pressed, your praise for having myself telephoned to Mr A J F O'Reilly in America, at a certain juncture, a first probe of his availability unto the confederacy which has now come to pass.

Third, and thereabout, the pattern of Fitzwilton raced to its rapid prescription – that of an egregious entity wherein seven, and soon more, disjunct businesses are to be near-autonomous though consanguineous, under only apron control from the mother.[7]

Whatever about Basil's prose, it is not the kind of text a busy radio news reporter would like to be handed five minutes before air-time, and it is certainly not the kind of text that a would-be investor was likely to find encouraging. In the end, Basil was dissuaded from delivering the above report, though he makes it clear that he felt it superior to the one he read to the shareholders. Michael Walker says that 'the *Bones* sounded fairly hollow in the last few years. Many of us thought – by God I wish he'd write something sensible but not carry on with this play-acting and producing those reports which we got the awful feeling were for his own entertainment rather than for the company's good'. Derek Hill enjoyed Basil's reports, but says that the board did 'take him to task' on a number of occasions and in particular when the company had had a bad year, when it was felt that his 'Gouldingese' humour was inappropriate. But Basil, according to many of his friends, could not understand why. Jim McCarthy remarks dryly that 'the *Chairman's Bones* were not a particularly good advertisement for Fitzwilton'.

Dr O'Reilly is somewhat kinder than many in his assessment of Basil's business skills. 'He was a whimsical businessman. He had an insight into it but he was without stamina for it. But he did broker one of the best deals ever for W & H M Goulding when we started Fitzwilton. I'm sure it would have gone bankrupt in 1975 had Basil not put together the deal he did in 1972. He was perceived as a welcome eccentric – a man to the manor born. He had his supporters but no real detractors. He didn't attract them because he wasn't from the same class as the average businessman. His *Chairman's Bones* was a celebrated literary event and was published in the *Financial Times*. The style was so prolix. He didn't really care much about the content of the *Bones* or about whether profits were up. In fact he never gave me any impression that he was interested in money at all. Basil was not a businessman within the meaning of the act. He was a businessman manqué, an amateur. No doubt he had great intelligence but he wasn't trained for anything. He epitomised that glorious amateurism.'

Valerie acknowledges that Basil's business behaviour, his *Bones* and his antics 'amused some and infuriated others. They considered that he didn't take his business seriously. People used to write to him asking him was he serious, but I don't think that it did the business any harm. The board did ask him not to write his reports the way he did, and that, I think, annoyed him. But what nearly finished him was when he went to a governors' meeting of the Bank of Ireland on a pair of roller skates. Basil said that the fellow in the top hat at the door was horrified when he asked him to park them. There was no amusement when he got into the boardroom. They just looked at him. Somebody in a real deadpan voice said "I believe you arrived on skates". I was amused by that sort of thing, and by the frog that he often wore on his dinner jacket. I thought people who disliked him because of it rather silly. The waiters

contd p169

Valerie showing off the new hydrotherapy pool at the Goatstown clinic.

The Tánaiste, Seán McEntee, stands next to Valerie at the opening of the sheltered workshop at Goatstown in 1964.

The president of the Order of Malta, Mr Noel Peart, Valerie, her brother, Gilbert Viscount Monckton of Brenchley, and Sir James Saville OBE.

Lady Valerie, Canon Cathal McCarthy, Mr Boyd Dunlop and staff at the opening of the first therapeutic pool at the Central Remedial Clinic in Goatstown.

Valerie 'cheating' during one of the CRC's 'Jimmy Saville charity walks'.

Princess Grace of Monaco arriving at Dublin Airport where she was met by Lord Killanin, Valerie and Charles and Máirín Haughey. Princess Grace attended a ball at Powerscourt House, held to raise funds for the CRC.

Valerie with Bing Crosby and his wife. The couple attended a fundraising dinner for the CRC.

*George Annesley, President de Valera
and Valerie at the opening of the
Central Remedial Clinic at Vernon
Avenue, Clontarf, in 1968.*

Valerie 'walking the plank'.

Valerie, President Childers and Jimmy Saville at Áras an Uachtaráin.

Valerie, President de Valera, a young thalidomide victim and the minister for health, Seán Flanagan, at the opening of the new CRC building in Clontarf in 1968.

President de Valera talks to children at the opening of the new CRC in 1968.

The minister for health Seán Flanagan, Geraldine Cruess-Callaghan and Valerie at the opening of the Central Remedial Clinic, Clontarf, in 1968.

Kevin McClory, Valerie and Charles Haughey during their fundraising trip to the United States.

Like his father, Lingard had a passionate interest in racing. He is seen here participating in a race in the Phoenix Park.

Ham Goulding was first officer on the Aer Lingus flight that took Valerie and Mary Cosgrave, daughter of the Taoiseach, on a fundraising trip to the United States in 1975. Left to right: Ham Goulding, Valerie, Mrs Cosgrave, Mr Liam Cosgrave, Mrs Geraldine Cruess-Callaghan, Dr Barbara Stokes and Ms Mary Cosgrave.

Valerie with Richard Harris. The actor was in Dublin for a charity show at the Gaiety Theatre.

Children collecting for the CRC in the early days.

Billy Sugrue with Valerie in the early 1950s. Billy is now married with two children and works for the CRC as a receptionist.

Valerie with some young students at a function for the National Council for the Elderly in 1994.

The Fitzwilton Building. Basil planned every detail with the architects and later chose all the fittings. Many Goulding employees found it uncomfortable and impractical to work in.

Basil in his thirties.

Jack and Maureen Lynch at the opening of the Jack B Yeats centenary exhibition in September 1971. Mr and Mrs Lynch are enjoying 'My Beautiful, My Beautiful', Valerie's favourite painting, which she later sold to Dr Tony O'Reilly.

One of Valerie's favourite photographs of Basil.

Valerie and Noel Keogh, who was head gardener at Dargle.

One of Basil's garden sculptures at Dargle Cottage.

Dargle Cottage.

Valerie receiving an Honorary Doctorate of Laws from University College Dublin. On Valerie's right is the writer Mary Lavin. President Éamon de Valera is seated.

Valerie at UNIFIL headquarters in Najuora, southern Lebanon, after her rescue by Irish Army personnel in August 1983. She had been trapped during a period of intense shelling. The trip to Beirut with John Bellingham of the Order of Malta (on the far right) was to assess the possibility of an Irish mission to help handicapped children there.

contd from p152

always laughed, even if the establishment didn't think it was funny. After he retired I think he was hurt by those who said "it all goes to show" when the company went under. I suppose some people were quite pleased that it happened'.

Anyone who knew Basil has a story about his antics. Jim McCarthy remembers Basil telling him that he was going to grow half a beard and half a moustache. The idea was to go into a restaurant and watch people looking at him. People would say 'Look, Basil's grown a beard' because he would hide the moustache with his hand. Then their companion would look over and see that he had grown a moustache because he would cover the beard side and reveal the moustache. 'Basil didn't just dye his hair odd colours, he would put a green stripe right down the centre of it. He was a terrible noticebox; he'd often go under the table in a restaurant and put his feet up on the chair so that when the waiter came all they would see was a pair of legs. I think he was mocking the world. He was the original practical joker.' But how, asks Michael Walker, 'can you take a man with a streak of green in his hair seriously? How can you regard him as a businessman? Basil's surface was a charade. But what was happening underneath?' Basil's friend, Jack Good, says that he was a man who was 'happier in the company of unorthodox people'. 'I remember Basil at a party with a stain in the middle of his tie, and he had a big arrow pointing it out with the word STAIN written on it. That kind of thing threw people. There was a touch of the showman there. He just didn't like being thought of as a stuffy, boring baronet.' Geraldine Cruess-Callaghan says Basil was a 'real trickster. Before we'd go on holidays he'd get tricks and joke things in London. You'd find a dog's turd on the side of your lettuce. One year he came to a Christmas party with a bun on the back of his head. It was full of his own hair clippings. But I do remember my husband saying that shareholders mightn't be too pleased to see their chairman running around with a frog on his shoulder or appearing at meetings on skates'.

Ham acknowledges that 'there was a body of opinion that my father was frivolous, that he wasn't a serious player. But he had this way of expressing things that was wrapped up in double meanings and he injected humour into serious issues which made what he said discountable as the ravings of an upper-class idiot'. Lingard rejects completely the suggestion that Basil was regarded as mad in some circles. 'My father was bored by the mundane. He was highly original and he liked to look at things from different angles. He was a lateral thinker. He was so far from mad: he was a man with a highly analytical mind. He viewed things dispassionately and objectively. He was highly radical and never given to rash judgement that was emotive.' Tim says that his father was trying to 'slough or shed the skin of the Protestant ascendancy world from which he came. He was at home with architects and anyone who could talk that language. He was an unconventional gardener so he was only slightly at home with them. But he was at home with anything to do with sport. I often wonder why he spent such a lot of time with conventional people, given his unconventional views on so many things. Maybe he was trying to get away from it, but it was part of his background and he had to go back to it. He liked to be a rebel in this conventional world, but he wouldn't have been a rebel had he lived in another world. His behaviour is only outrageous because of the staid kind of world in which he operated'. Perhaps the best judgement on Basil's business acumen can be found in the fact that he claimed he would like to appoint Jimmy Saville, whom he admired greatly, to the board of Fitzwilton. Madman or genius?

Basil played on many stages and apparently drew immense pleasure from the performances, whether they were on the sports field or in the appreciation of art or the making of a garden. With Dr James White he founded the Contemporary Irish Arts Society. 'He was a most remarkable man – a man of great integrity and character: not a libertine type but a man of consistency and humour. He appeared Bohemian in the world of Dublin but he was consistently moral and had a view of life based on high standards. He was by nature artistic and could make woodwork, a natural gardener, and he knew about sculpture and art. He wasn't hard enough to be a highly successful businessman: he was a highly civilised man who was in business. Like W B Yeats he regarded the spiritual as the most important element of life. He expressed his world through his writing, and like Joyce and Beckett he used expression that was never boringly repetitive. He preferred unorthodox solutions and that applied to his life and to his house, furniture, his surroundings and his approach. He understood and was attracted to the double meaning of words in Joyce and Beckett and lived in that world of curious dualism that they were part of. Basil was a businessman and part of the conventional world, but as a gesture of resistance to joining that conventional world he skates to meetings. I think he would have put off some men by the angularity of his views. He'd put off the golf club types and the drinking set – people who talk a certain way to emphasise their maleness in case anyone might think them homosexual. But it would be wrong to say he wasn't normal or to attribute homosexuality because of his style. He was attractive to women and he had a natural masculinity and femininity, but he was developed on both sides. I think that if Basil met someone and loved them, he would not have had a problem exploring it sexually. He was intellectual and high-minded, and not bedevilled by his sexuality. He had a freer approach to life and would have been more inclined to be moved by real feelings than by sheer experimentation.'

Basil met the painter Robert Ballagh through his son Tim when the pair hung out in Toner's pub in Dublin. Basil enjoyed Ballagh's art and commissioned him to work on the new Goulding headquarters. The Fitzwilton building, like many things connected with Basil, was controversial. Ballagh says 'He had a wide appreciation of art and moved easily from the classics to the moderns, but he lived in the modern world and was fascinated with elements of contemporary art which I would describe as romantic modernism. That style is exemplified by artists such as Barrie Cooke and Camille Souter, both of whom Basil encouraged and supported. On the international stage that style is represented by an artist like Antoni Tapis. The style is very textured and fluid. But he also liked my work and I think there it was the inherent humour that appealed to him. His taste was wide but he did prioritise his collection, and by and large his purchases centred on romantic modernism. The core of his collection was ruled by an emotional response to pictures, where a collector like his friend Gordon Lambert had a rigorously rational and intellectual response to art and the collection reflected that.'

In 1961 Dr White, the curator of the Municipal Gallery, mounted an exhibition of a selection of Basil's paintings. Entitled *One Man's Meat*, it was mainly an exhibition of living Irish artists 'painting with non-figurative intentions' and included work by Patrick Collins, Patrick Scott, Barrie Cooke, Gerard Dillon, Patrick Hickey, Cecil King, Norah McGuinness, Leslie McSweeney, Eric Patton, Nano Reid, Anna Ritchie, Noel Sheridan and Camille Souter. He also included his important collection of paintings by Oscar Kokoschka, Jack B Yeats and a tapestry by Jean Lurcat. In his curator's introduction Dr White said that the Municipal Gallery was 'deeply conscious that contemporary Irish painting is poorly represented in our collection. Sir Basil's pictures by living Irish artists do much to rectify that situation. Furthermore, they indicate in their owner a courageous mind and a capacity, almost unique, of anticipating talent amongst the up and coming painters. It is therefore a double benefit that we can show in this exhibition, not only expressionist masterpieces, but a fine and comprehensive coverage of what may well prove to be the significant movement of this period in Ireland'.[8]

Dr White says that Basil's collection showed a strong 'taste for expressionist landscapes in work by Yeats and Kokoschka. That taste was based on his own interest in nature and in his way of seeing things and his imagination. Yeats goes beyond the visible to introduce the spiritual in line with his brother, W B Yeats. The connection is immediate. All the paintings in that collection were comparatively abstract but they all move out into the area of landscapes or subject paintings which move from the present into an imaginative idea. Basil's taste grew out of that world of Joyce, Beckett and Yeats. In general he wasn't a collector of artists from other countries, but he did express his taste in buying Kokoschka, which is German expressionism. Expressionism is the form which expresses the artist's desire to use shape, form and colour to emphasise the emotional expression rather than the intellectual or physical appearance. Basil carried that expressionism into his writing. I believe that he got all his spiritual uplift and expression through works of art and from nature in his garden, whereas Valerie got it through her work for the handicapped'.

Tim does not agree that his father's approach to art was purely emotional, and emphasises that Basil's response was 'an amalgam of emotion and intellect'. Writing about Basil's appreciation of art when the collection was being sold, Tim said that his father had been his finest art teacher:

> He enjoyed wildly dissimilar works, always ready to express their impact and explain their 'stagecraft'. Above all lay his insistence on quality within an idiom. He wrote 'It is not the idioms that count; it is the performance within one'. And 'Quality is by far the senior ingredient over idiom. When idiom and quality fuse you get impact'. This is not to say that he eschewed the initial sensual output. He was your real arts'n science man, able to marry intellect with emotion . . . .
>
> Maybe why he vibrated so harmoniously with contemporary art and artists was that he was an artist of calibre himself. His mediums were diverse; gardening, architecture, flower arrangement, cabinet making, industrial design and words, to name but a few. His remarkable articulacy on visual matters was fed, no doubt, from these variant disciplines. He shot his word-pictures with artillery from them, and also from his business and sporting life. Art became a ski-slope, perspective a stuffed-shirt business man, colour a ravishing mistress whose charms could lead to perdition. A shower of allusions were planted around that which couldn't be spoken, enhancing its significance for us listeners and readers.
>
> Here was an early champion of non-figurative art quite at home in turning convention on its head and welcoming surprise. He embraced the incomprehensible, urging us to see its poetry rather than flatten it with the hammer of comprehension. He once commenced an article on art appreciation, 'There is much to be said for not understanding modern art. For one thing you can enjoy it more'. This was followed by pages of pure 'Basilese' which to him was as plain as day but to many as dense as plum pudding. Who could match his powerstrokes of prose or irreverent jauntiness on the most serious of subjects? What remains is the indelible influence of a man who was, if you forgive filial attachment, 'a master of all trades, jack of none'.

Valerie says that she doesn't know where Basil developed his interest in art. 'His mother didn't like paintings and neither did I until I saw the Jack B Yeats painting, *My Beautiful, My Beautiful*. That was one I wanted, and from then on I was interested.' Rosemary Garvey tells the story that Basil bought the painting because it was the first time that Valerie had shown any interest in painting, though he wasn't sure 'which she liked best, the picture or the horse'.[9] After Basil's death, when Valerie sold much of the collection, Tim did a copy of *My*

Beautiful, My Beautiful, which now hangs in Valerie's bungalow in Dargle. The original was bought by Dr O'Reilly following a valuation by James White. It hangs in the entrance hall at Castlemartin and beside it is the Jack B Yeats letter to Valerie, sent after the painting was purchased. Valerie says that she hopes that Basil had 'no inkling that I'd have to sell [the collection]. I'd promised him that I'd take care of the gardens. But I think it was the collecting that diminished our money. He had collected the most incredible number of well-known people. He couldn't resist buying and I don't blame him, but it did mean problems. But we had to sell or the boys would have had no money. It wasn't until afterwards, after he died, when I read through our papers, that I realised that he must have been in trouble in the last ten to fifteen years'.

As chairman of the Contemporary Irish Art Society and member of the Arts Council, Basil's love of art was not just a private thing. He was involved in policies and decisions that were regarded as highly controversial by many artists at the time. Bobby Ballagh remembers the period well, though he emphasises that he does not feel that Basil personally excluded any artist from the number of those who were actively promoted by the art establishment. 'That establishment did disgraceful things, though I was friendly with them. There was an exclusiveness and elitism in the way that power was exercised in the art world. The entire emphasis of the Arts Council, under the directorship of Fr Donal O'Sullivan, was on contemporary visual arts, and they didn't support any other art form. They supported a select coterie within that and there were very good artists who fell outside that coterie and whose careers were in the doldrums as a result. But they did believe that they were bringing great art to the Philistines, and so the non-believers were treated with contempt. There was a certain section of contemporary artists who were perceived as representing the true faith, but the people who were left out have very strong feelings about it.

'I believe it was an authoritarian council. Basil was an ordinary member of it but I think it would be naïve to think that he didn't take part in these decisions. Some of my colleagues would have hated him, and the things I liked and loved about him would have been seen by them as symbols of a decaying aristocracy, dilettantish and all that.

James McKenna wrote a play poking fun at the art establishment – and the fertiliser business featured in it. You'd often hear an older artist say "did you hear Basil has bought such and such a picture". And someone would say "it's not the first time he bought shit". The connection was made between his fertiliser business and his art'. Bobby Ballagh feels that Basil made a significant contribution to the contemporary Irish art scene in his personal support of artists like Cooke, Souter and himself and 'simply by putting his hand in his pocket and buying. But nowadays there is nobody about on the art scene with his sense of fun. There's nobody with the leg-pulling and humour that he injected. Whenever Basil comes into my mind he is always smiling'.

When Basil left Fitzwilton he could hardly have been described as someone who would lack for something to do: apart from his art there was his internationally known garden, his carpentry, squash, tennis, skiing, the piano accordion and his interest in jazz. And yet there is a sense that he lacked a certain purpose despite his many protestations that he would have much to do. The evidence of his need to communicate can be found in the writing projects which he undertook and the considerable attempts he made to be published. He published *Alpha Basil – A Business Alphabet* in 1976, and according to the *Cork Examiner* review it was, 'witty and very much to the point, this is for all businessmen and union men too . . . . The book is full of delightful quotes. Get a few copies and send them out as presents. Much better than smoked salmon, less expensive and a great deal more valuable'. Basil's entry under the letter T might perhaps have been influenced by his recent experience with Fitzwilton:

> T is for Takeover. Takeover is the racey form of acquisition – in turn the posh word for buying. It is so racey that it sometimes has to be termed a merger: but fine-tuning can arrange for it to be called a reverse takeover.
>
> Takeovers have the advantage over acquisitions of setting up a presumption of sinful motivations: whereas acquisitions are termed rationalisations, takeovers are lucky to be termed ungentlemanly.
>
> From this there may be observed a distinction with or without a difference, namely between people thrown out of irreplacability as consequence of a racey takeover and people thrown out of irreplacability as a consequence of a gentlemanly acquisition.

Another thing not to cerebrate about much is whether the takeover is an extension or an expansion of the taker's business. Tidiness is to untidiness as gray is to grey. The smart mot on the matter is that it depends.

What it depends on, if you ask, are real capacities of analysis and judgement: these are about as natural and simple as green chartreuse.

Many a somnolent business has been redeemed by an overtaker from the undertaker; and natural dread of change in habitudes gives a takeover man wonderful opportunity to relieve it.

In Basil's papers there are many examples of doggerel such as:

In all of the conventual immurities
They teach of the value of purities:
And the value of mon
Isn't second to nun
In the school of Fitzwilliam Securities

as well as witty pen pictures and serious observations dealing with subjects as diverse as the architectural merits of the controversial Central Bank in Dublin's Dame Street, his views on the proper writing of the chairman's report and two substantial pieces on religion and his impending death. He worked very hard to have his *99 Articles* or *A Hayride through the corn-fields of Religion* published, though he was repeatedly turned down by both agents and publishers. He had a long correspondence with Penguin Books, who advised him that it took so long to 'concentrate on your prose acrobatics that in my case I have long since lost your meaning'.[10] Penguin concluded that 'the material does not look promising, as an economic proposition'. But Basil was not put off. He repeatedly re-wrote parts of the *99 Articles* and showed sections of it to Archdeacon McCarthy, who had remained a family friend after Valerie's conversion. One can but wonder about Basil's purpose when considering the following on the subject of contraception:

Some folk – usually nice ones – cling to Prayer as being God's Do-it-Himself abortifacient, though their way of putting it is rather less specific. But one has to hand it to Religion for having so sufficiently got past the recommendation of Prayer as a reliable regulator as to be found now prescribing the Billings method as more effective – though the claim is no walk-over! Both methods however, carry the essential instruction 'abstention' – along with the somewhat pathetic assurance that 'Abstinence makes the heart grow fonder'. This is, of course, a sad misquotation of the correct dictum 'Abstinence makes the male go yonder'.

On page 190 we find the following on sex:

> Both Religion and Ethics have Sex on their hands as a big tease; but also in their hands as a big stick. And so basically have people always had Sex on their minds that the genteel notion of the virgin-birth issued by Religion (see Mary), was accepted with acclamation, and thus has, ever since, remained the Magic Circle's best-selling presentation of Sex.
>
> Religion's handling of the tease has always been first, to invest their clients with the sure presumption of guilt and therefore sinfulness; to market, then, the anodynes of Confession and Penance; to under-force (cf. reinforce) these with the caution that their shelf-life is very short; and to stand by for further fragilities.

On page 69 under the heading of Doctrine/Dogma Basil observes that:

> the splendid attainments of Dogma were topped, in medieval times, by the staggering Miracle of Transubstantiation; and finally and fully fortified by the achievement of two further world-titles – the proclamation in 1854, of the Immaculacy of Mary, and, in 1870, of the Infallibility of the Pope.
>
> The latter, interestingly or not, is a hook-back to the original *ipse dixit* of the Pythagoreans: whatever their master said was final. And whether or not one fawns upon Infallibility there is this simple thing to be said about it; that it is logical in the circumstances. For it is the other side of the coin Dogma. If the marching order is to be ineluctable then the authority for it must be infallible.

It is possible to look on Basil's attempt to deal with the big themes as his response to finding himself outside of the world he had occupied for more than forty years. Tim feels that the only time his father was depressed was in the period after he was forced out of Fitzwilton. 'I remember him sitting at the table and saying that he wished he could die. I was very shocked. He did get better after that but it was then that he wrote the A–Z or the *99 Articles*. It was very bitterly put and not, I think, publishable. I wrote an A–Z of self-realisation in reply. I wrote it out by hand and illustrated it. It was meant to be the other side of things. I was saying that religion may be off the wall, but self-realisation and spirituality is a different story.'

According to Dr O'Reilly, the Fitzwilton saga did not affect Basil's composure. 'It didn't affect him at all. His sense of his own grandeur was unconnected with the esteem of the business community. The fact that he was talked about was sufficient reward for him.' Billy Milne disagrees: 'Basil was an expansionist. So the Fitzwilton debacle was a reversal of fortune'. But the man who had the best opportunity of observing Basil's demeanour in the period after his removal from Fitzwilton was the man with whom he shared his garden, Noel Keogh. Noel had begun working in Basil's garden when he was still a teenager, and over a period of nearly twenty-five years the two men had spent many an hour in each other's company. 'It was a big blow to him. I could see it in him. To my estimation he was devastated. He didn't say it but I could read between the lines. I did think he was depressed. He wasn't the same bubbly man.'

Basil's most meaningful prose was, perhaps, *The Canyon and I*, written after he was told that he was suffering from liver cancer. While retaining much of the style and humour of his other efforts, there is a great sense in *The Canyon and I* that, at last, Basil had realised that life was more than just a stage. Basil was already very seriously ill before the family explained to him that he had cancer; and while any feeling of how he reacted to this information largely depends on his interaction with family and friends, and their consequent view of his view, it would appear that there is a consensus of opinion that he grew in the experience of relinquishing life.

Ham was with Basil and Valerie on a skiing holiday in Verbier in February 1981 when the first indications of Basil's illness appeared. 'Verbier was the last holiday. I remember the moment so well because what happened was so unusual for him. The whole party had been skiing all day and I was just outside a restaurant at the top of the hill when they all said let's do another run. My father said that he was tired and that he'd stay and have a cup of tea. Even though he was in his seventies he never said that sort of thing. Afterwards when I realised he was so ill it stood out as the first moment that I saw it affect him.' According to Lingard, Basil's doctor thought straight away that it was liver cancer but didn't tell him. 'Either Dad was incredibly slow on the uptake or he didn't want to know. He went into St Michael's for a bowel operation and he hoped that he would get over it very quickly.' Close friends received copies of the following note prepared by Basil on the eve of his operation on 31 April 1981:

Practical Hints for Surgeon as to Operation on 'Room 12'

1. Ensure that X-rays are displayed right way up. This will obviate patient being laid on belly and entry made through back.

2. Ensure no confusion of X-rays with the case in Room 12A of the excessive breeder. I expect to generate more children.

3. Inform the anaesthetist beforehand that her lunch is being kept hot for her and will not spoil.

4. Do not use hairpins or curlers for joining tubes: the final 'sew-up' count can thus be confusing, and may embarrass theatre-nurses. Same applies to attractive nail-scissors.

5. Do not allow your pride, should there be applause around the theatre for the brilliance of your operation, to make you feel that an encore is called for – so that, with a few deft strokes, you whip out an appendix or the like.

6. Don't forget your lunch is getting cold

Issued by B. G. 'the day before'.

In *The Canyon and I*, Basil lays out his account of how he came to understand that he was going to die:

At the time I retired from business a journalist who was interviewing me for a leading newspaper article asked me, *inter alia*, 'What is your ambition now?' I replied that it was to ski down Mount Gele at the age of 70. That peak is the highest in Verbier, and rough on rats. In the spring of last year I did it, and others too.

But this year, in Verbier, though I skied Mont Gele again I felt flaccid by times – didn't want to go out skiing, hung around the hotel on the count that there was bad visibility today, it would probably be fine tomorrow.

And I finished the tour by losing my attack and feeling thoroughly out on the descent of the Gran St Bernard Pass. I felt a bit like the coming of bleak winter after a lovely mellow autumn.

And when I came home my tennis got steadily worse, both in nimbleness and in sighting. My regular Sunday buddies must have noticed it, maybe commented 'Basil was a bit off today', but they were too chummy to rub my nose in it.

Why did I have the stomach operation a bit later? I honestly have found it hard to remember. My wife tells me that it was because my ejection system was getting jammed.

The point about this forgetting is that it illustrates how I never suspected a thing, except of course some little blockage.

And when the operation was over and the excellent surgeon told me that he had removed a foot of tubing (colon) from the about 21 feet that one has, my pellucid innocence thought no more than that the blockage was gone; I'd be playing tennis better in a few weeks.

And so it looked for a fortnight or so. Full of attack I was; visited my tennis buddies, watched them, drank with them, went home late for lunch with a 'See you . . . '

But then a sort of stiffness, a constriction, above the belly, came across me; and each day it wasn't better tomorrow as I had expected it to be.

Our local GP came a couple of times; then the third time he said, 'I think you ought to go at once to a man in London I've enquired about. He's quite a specialist in liver complaints'.

So my wife and I set off for the Westminster Hospital and The Professor.

He put me in a ward with a cold-buffet of patients who looked to me ghastly ill. A bit depressing, it seemed, for one who was as healthy as I.

Strolling down the passage, for exercise, on the second day, I said to my wife 'I've just thought of something rather obvious to ask the Professor: it's 'what does he think my trouble is?'

In panic, I learned later, she phoned The Professor to forewarn him. When he came in the next day I thought to myself how pleasantly attentive he was. We talked of this and that for a while – until I said 'Oh, by the way, there is something I forgot to ask you . . . . '

'Since you are intelligent and courageous,' he said, 'I'll tell you'.

So he did.

One thing was plain; I wasn't intelligent.

Ham was in St Michael's with his mother after Basil's bowel operation. 'I remember after the operation, after they'd opened him up and they'd seen enough and my mother said "he's going to die". I was very upset and began to cry. She was very calm. I suppose it was internalised with her.' Valerie is not comfortable talking about feelings and emotions and is therefore terse in her remarks about Basil's last months. 'Even when Basil was sixty-nine and seventy he played tennis like mad and then suddenly he looked tired. First he had a prostate operation and he didn't really get better from that. Then another minor operation, and then the doctor said he had cancer. We didn't tell him. We went to Westminster Hospital because Basil's brother Ossian recommended it. He got chemotherapy there. All it did was make him sick. I promised him that his hair wouldn't be affected. I was a senator at the time and there was an election but I pulled out of everything including the clinic. I don't know if that was a good thing or not. He had approved of euthanasia, and though he must have known that he was going to die for three or four months, he tried to go on living. It was most interesting for someone with his views. Up to the last month he thought he would pull through. Part of the time he spent trying to stop the pain and sickness and convince himself that there wasn't any pain. He couldn't read and didn't really want to be read to – but he did want someone with him. He died shortly after Christmas. We didn't know what to do, but we did get him downstairs on the day. I couldn't give him a Christmas present – all I had was an old tatty bit of paper on which I wrote – "Just to let you know that I love you". Then he died. It was easy. It took about three days. We were all sitting there and I think it was Lingard who said "I think he's dead".'

According to Tim, Basil began writing *The Canyon and I* a few days after he was told he had terminal cancer. 'I don't believe my mother liked it and afterwards I don't think that she wanted it to be published. He had not known previously that he had cancer, and he wrote about the feelings he experienced when he was told. My ex-wife Annie played an important role during Dad's illness. She was an angel. We went up to Dargle to stay with them but it was on false pretences. I pretended that I was painting, which I was, but we were there because we knew he was dying. I found it difficult that we didn't tell him. I was the one who disagreed, but I was wrong, because Dad said he preferred not to know. After the operation they just sewed him back up. Annie cooked for him, which was very important because with liver cancer his taste went. I remember him saying that there was nothing left that he could enjoy, food, gardening or reading: "The only things left to me are things of beauty". So I propped up pictures at the end of his bed and he was able to look at them.

'While there, I was working on an exhibition of paintings of his garden; it turned into an exhibition of the river as well. In the last nine months of Dad's life I painted fifty pictures of the Dargle. I sat outside all that summer and at first he would wander out and look, and then later on when he was bed-bound I brought them in each day to his bedroom. We'd talk about them and he would give a critique. The exhibition opened on 8 January 1982 and he died on the sixteenth. But Ham videoed the opening and Basil was able to see it. He was delighted. I lived out one side of life that he would have liked. But everyone had their own language with him. We communicated through a Beckettian language: with Ham there was the flying and with Ling he would talk about racing. He'd been to some of the great races in the 1930s. He was one of the last Renaissance people I'd met. He was a classicist with a good knowledge of Latin and Greek. He was interested in science and technology and he was a great sportsman, artist, gardener and businessman. But the language we spoke and the way we communicated was through the painting.'

Basil often asked to see Noel Keogh and his wife Loretta during his last days. Noel had been the gardener at Dargle since his late teens. He feels that Basil knew he had cancer quite early on but chose not to share that knowledge. He remembers meeting Basil just after he had come out of hospital around Easter time. 'Sir Basil said to me – "It's time for a walk". He talked about x-rays and didn't exactly say that the news was bad, but he did say that what had happened was "like a brick between the eyes". Then he started talking to me about looking after the garden for him. Then I knew.' Even in his very last hours Noel says Basil talked to him about what they should plant next. Loretta Keogh remembers that Basil sent word with Noel that he would like to see her. Going up the drive from her gate lodge she was tearful at the prospect of seeing Basil, a man that she loved like a father, about to die. 'When I got into the room he had a check shirt and his Arran sweater on and he looked better than I had expected. He broke the ice by straight away asking me about the part-time job I had in the January sales. And we joked about how it was no life. He made it okay for me instead of the other way round. Then Lady Goulding came in and said he might need to rest. That was the last time I saw him – three days before he died.'

Basil was deeply loved by his daughter-in-law Annie, and though the product of a very different class and generation, she felt that she grew very close to him while she nursed him though his last months. 'He had an Edwardian education. He was quite a formal person in many ways but at heart he was affectionate but not overtly. All Basil's life he had been trained not to show his emotions. The boys were the same in many ways. But I think he changed enormously during his illness. Valerie needed our help because she found it so painful. Often at dinner she'd get a migraine or something and she'd have to go to bed. Then Tim and myself would go up to Basil. I think he might have felt lonely or cut off without us. I did a lot of things with him that he really enjoyed. We planted a whole bank of the garden with buds. He knew he wouldn't see them but he wanted to do it. I brought him into town to some exhibitions. I remember we went upstairs in the John Taylor Gallery and had tea. There was a series of lithographs by Patrick Hickey that represented the months of the year. They were lovely and Basil got all excited. Even though he had stopped buying then because he couldn't afford it anymore, he bought one – a picture of a dried artichoke. I thought it was wonderful that when all his other senses went, when he could no longer enjoy his food, when the sports were all gone, that he could still enjoy the paintings. He used to be so precise about where things should be placed, and if he saw something that wasn't just so, he'd move it. Once when I was in the bedroom and he saw something out of place and I went to readjust it for him, he stopped me and said that it didn't matter anymore. But he said it in a happy sense. 'That side of him was all gone. He had let go of his attachments. He died in a very beautiful way. He was in his home surrounded by his family. It was wonderful that he was able to let go of many things before he died – able to die happily and gracefully. He let go of the extraneous and was at one with his spirit.'

In *The Canyon and I*, Basil looked at his own experience and rationalisation of death and confronted his impending reality with his previously held views on religion, ethics, morals and euthanasia. Describing the tract as his 'own home-movie' he offered the world a copy.

Now the consequence of Death is rather less uncertain to the unreligious, though this is surprising to the religious. For if – a mordant but not a morbid pronouncement, this – you are, on Death, a pebble on a beach, washed smooth (as a matter of poesy only) to the tides, then you possess the ideal dualism of, on the one hand, certainly avoiding all the miseries of life and, on the other, certainly not missing any of the pleasures.

A Jesuit could not do better: hasn't.

That's what I would have written at that point. But later I thought that the principle needed proper elevation, should not just be buried in the coffin of a *passant* sentence.

So I elevated it into a tract which I fancied pinned to the door of some notional cathedral. There it looked like this:

The Smoothed Pebble

And be thou of unruffled good cheer that at thy last day thou shalt attain to the perfect inertia of the Smoothed Pebble, as on the beach, washed by the tides of time: or failing that, to some other morsel of garbage, less poetic but as inert.

No worry nor misery of human existence shalt there ever more be for thee; for these shall be entirely unfelt. Neither shall any pleasure or joy obtrude; for their absence shall also be entirely unfelt.

So that they who remain to grieve most shall grieve only from the pangs of the past and the parting; and may cling to the ideal of reposing one day on the same beach – together.

Basil was a 'narcissist' to some, 'the best actor that never went on the stage' to another and 'like a brother' to one former friend and employee. Fitzwilton director Vincent Ferguson wrote this poem which was carried in the *Irish Independent* the day after Basil died.

For Basil

True Hedonist, taking pleasure in
Everything he touched, nature, art, words,
Sharing his beautiful vision
With generous spirit.
Opening our mundane eyes to ordinary wonders.
Life is a ski-run
With excitement, danger, beauty, rushing past,
Adrenalin flowing,
Eternally young,
He soars;
We look on, leaden-footed, with amazement,
Gratitude – and love.

As he slipped away into a coma Basil looked around the room: 'Everything is perfect,' he said.

1 The Saturday Interview, *The Irish Times*, 2 August 1975.
2 *The Irish Times*, 18 January 1982.
3 *A Short History of the Firm W & H M Goulding Limited From Its Foundation in 1856, Its Development To The Present Day And Its Plans For The Future*. Courtesy of Derek Hill.
4 *Ibid*.
5 The Saturday Interview, *The Irish Times*, 2 August 1975.
6 *Ibid*.
7 Unpublished text in Lady Goulding's possession.
8 Curator's introduction to *One Man's Meat*, Sir Basil Goulding collection, November 1961.
9 Rosemary Garvey to Valerie, 10 July 1991.
10 Penguin editor, Michael Dover, to Basil, 29 March 1977.

8

A SOLDIER OF DESTINY

I was a Charlie woman, which I felt bad about, because it was Jack Lynch who got me in. But he wasn't the man who was going to be tough enough to run the country, so when it came to who was going to be the leader I did the dirt.

Valerie says that her preference for Fianna Fáil, which some might regard as quixotic given her background, was a result of the first coalition government's decision to abolish the External Relations Act of 1936 and the subsequent Declaration of the Republic in 1948. There are many unusual aspects to Valerie's view of this matter, not least the fact that she still harbours a belief that there is a future for a united Ireland within the Commonwealth. How, the reader might ask, can an avowed republican and passionate supporter of Charles Haughey despise a Fine-Gael led decision to abolish the last remaining link with Britain, while at the same time cherish the notion of an Ireland within the British Commonwealth of Nations? Valerie sees no conflict at all. It was the manner of the act rather than the act itself that she abhorred. 'John A Costello went off to Canada without saying a word to anyone. He didn't talk about the issue to the public. There was no referendum. He announced the declaration of the Republic in the middle of a dinner in Canada. It was a dirty trick. It's not the way that things should be done, without even asking. At least Fianna Fáil had always stated their colours.' In fact the Tánaiste, William Norton, had told the Dáil in August 1948 that 'it would do our national self-respect good both at home and abroad if we were to proceed without delay to abolish the External Relations Act'.[1] While Fine Gael had always been in favour of close Commonwealth ties, it was hoped that the abolition of what was derisively called the 'dictionary republic' and the adoption of a clear-cut constitutional position would 'take the gun out of politics'.[2]

Nonetheless, Valerie's reaction to John A Costello's address at a Canadian Bar Association dinner in September 1948 was shared by many who saw it as a volte-face and, as historian John A Murphy points out, 'there appeared to be grounds at the time for thinking that a crucially important constitutional decision had been made in an arbitrary fashion several thousand miles away. Many were astonished that the announcement had been made without any regard for diplomatic protocol, and were no less amazed at a Fine Gael change of policy which had not been aired at the general election seven months before. Not surprisingly, Fianna Fáil deputies were particularly critical'.[3] Charles Haughey is one of Valerie's heroes: he understands the reasoning behind Valerie's reaction to Costello's initiative. 'That reaction is in character. The way she would rationalise that, would be that Costello and Fine Gael did it for the wrong reasons – but Fianna Fáil are republicans and they make no bones about it. They are honest, whereas Costello was dishonest about what and why he did it.'

Valerie got her first sense of the rough and tumble of the hustings when she went to England during her father's campaign in Bristol West in 1951. Walter had been rejected at a selection convention two years previously by Oxford Conservatives who, when told that he had been through the divorce courts, received him in dead silence. Things improved for Walter in Bristol West, and he served the constituency until 1957. 'My father wasn't interested in politics though he was asked to do this and that. I think he wanted to settle back to being a barrister after the war, but Churchill wanted him in his Cabinet, so he asked him to become an MP. But the divorce was a problem and they turned him down in Oxford. He got in the second time, and directly he was elected he was right in the middle of it as Minister of Labour and National Service. I think it all nearly killed him. He was different from other Conservatives. He was a socialist at heart. He felt shaken by poverty.' But whatever about Valerie's view of the nature of her father's conservatism, there is no doubt that she enjoyed his election campaign. 'It was exciting and fun; all the hubbub and fighting. I remember asking Basil would he ever get involved and he said "never: it's dirty". Of course I felt that I couldn't get involved in politics because of the clinic. But I did change my mind.'

In 1977 Valerie decided to run for the Senate, taking the view that there was no impediment to her declaring her political affiliation for Fianna Fáil. In June, a few weeks before the general election, she wrote to Jack Lynch telling him of her intention to run. She was nominated by the clinic and would seek votes on the administrative panel. Valerie's political move coincided with an attempt within Fianna Fáil to find women candidates. It wasn't an easy task. At that time, many high-profile women were involved in activities that were an anathema to Fianna Fáil and all it then stood for. Another difficulty was that it was not easy to get women candidates through selection conventions. A case in point was Mary Harney, who despite the imprimatur of Jack Lynch, could not get through the selection conventions in her own constituency, and had to be imposed on Dublin South East in 1977. Lynch was looking for more than just women candidates; he wanted to broaden the base and profile of the party and get away from the hack image of the Taca[4] money-men and their mohair suits. According to one senior Fianna Fáil adviser at the time, the fact that Valerie had close links with Charles Haughey was not an issue for Jack Lynch. She was a woman with the kind of profile that the party needed.

According to Valerie, she knew, even before her election campaign was over, that if she didn't make it, Lynch would appoint her to the Senate as one of his Taoiseach's eleven nominees. 'I kept campaigning and I nearly got in on my own. I really would have preferred to have got in myself, and I remember at the count, all my campaign workers were telling me that I was in. I couldn't pretend that I knew that I was in anyway.' When the list of those who were nominated by the Taoiseach was announced, Valerie was in the west of Ireland staying with her friend Rosemary Garvey, in a very remote place beyond Louisburgh. Rosemary's neighbour Mary O'Malley heard the news on the radio and cycled over to tell Valerie the good news. According to Rosemary, Valerie was very excited and threw her arms around her in delight. Another of the Taoiseach's nominees at the time says that Valerie's appointment 'was symbolic because of the clinic and because she was a woman. If she'd been a man running the CRC she would not have been appointed. They were looking for women from across the board. Lynch and Cosgrave both had an old-fashioned notion that upper-class people were an asset in the Senate'.[5] It is difficult to assess whether Valerie completely understood the reasoning behind her nomination. 'If you think about it, it was ridiculous of Jack Lynch to come and say to me that he was going to put me in, an Englishwoman with a title. Unless, of course, he was more clever than I thought.'

Valerie's platform had been totally identified with services for the handicapped. She told the journalist Mavis Arnold, 'We can no longer ignore the needs of the handicapped or continue to treat them as people from Mars. They represent something like two per cent of the population and these are only the ones we know about. I might only be one small voice speaking on their behalf, but at least it would be a start'. When she actually took her seat, Valerie realised very quickly that 'it would be very easy to make a big mistake. So I decided to listen. I didn't speak very often'. Eileen Cassidy was another of Jack Lynch's nominees. She had been chairman of the Fianna Fáil cumann in Ballymore, County Kildare. Lynch had heard her speak at an election rally, and though she was not a candidate, he offered her a nomination. Her initial meeting with Valerie was at the first post-election Fianna Fáil parliamentary meeting in Leinster House. 'I don't think that Valerie was even a member of Fianna Fáil until Eoin Ryan rang her and said it would be a good idea to join before she came to the parliamentary party meeting. We became friends because in ways we were the same. We sat together in the chamber and shared coffee breaks.' Eileen Cassidy is very fond of Valerie and enjoyed the intimacy that they shared while senators. However, she feels that Valerie 'was not a political animal. She hadn't come up in politics the rough way, and if you want to get on in politics you have to start at the county councils. Even I was resented because I didn't hold clinics. But she had no perception of the resentment that was felt amongst county councillors and failed candidates for whom the Senate was a means to a Dáil seat, and as a reward for those of the party faithful who had tried hard to win a difficult seat'. Eileen Cassidy says that Valerie was regarded by her fellow senators in the way 'they might look on an exotic bird of paradise in their midst. They walked around her gingerly'.

A critic who sat on the Fianna Fáil benches with Valerie says that she had 'a queen-like approach. People were intimidated by her. She came from a totally different background from everyone else in Leinster House, and it wasn't just that she was wealthier. She stuck out like a sore thumb. Most women in politics, whether elected or not, but particularly those that are nominated, are very forceful in terms of their ideas, they have to be to get through the system. Politics doesn't carry many women passengers. Valerie Goulding was the opposite. I used to wonder why the hell she was nominated. Everyone's view of her was probably the same as mine: a very nice person but why is she here. She didn't have political ideas or views. She was appointed because of her work outside politics, but she never became a politician. She wasn't able, even at a personal level, to disagree with people, and that didn't mean that she didn't disagree, but she wasn't able to do so personally and openly. She was so charming, but her life was about agreeing with people. That was good when she was working for the clinic. She was probably too old when she came into politics. Her personality didn't suit it – you can't be nice all of the time in politics'.

According to one of those involved in the selection of candidates at the time, there was disappointment that Valerie didn't make better use of her time in the Senate, given the opposition that existed at cumann level to the appointment of outsiders. The same source points out that elements within Fianna Fáil would have regarded Lynch's appointment of people like Mary Harney, Eileen Cassidy and Valerie Goulding, as further proof that he was 'going off the boil'. While agreeing with the view that her period in the Senate was not productive, Charles Haughey makes the point that it is very difficult for a 'backbencher to achieve anything, and even more difficult for a Senator. She didn't have good political cop – that's a long apprenticeship. And then she'd never get to the root of things the way I would, having been born here and reared here and having gone to school here. She wasn't a boon companion or a buddy but she was a popular and well-liked member of the party. It would be wrong to say she was an oddity. They took her just the way she was but they knew her background. She just wasn't one of the boys – or the girls!'

Valerie does not regard her period in the Senate as a success and regrets that it was not more constructive. She found herself sharing a room with Seán Doherty, Jackie Fahey and Martin Joe O'Toole. Martin says that Valerie was 'well able for the craic', though one can only guess at the scale of the chasm which would need to have been bridged for the three men to have found any common language with Valerie. She is reticent about her room-mates, though she admits that her relationship with Seán Doherty never got off the ground. Those who are critical of her failure to do something in the Senate, miss the point that for Valerie, being there was the goal. She regarded the office as 'a sort of PR job for the clinic'. In her mind it was simply the extension of the rest of her work, and she wasn't interested in other issues. More than likely she didn't appreciate that this would leave her open to considerable criticism when she moved onto the larger political stage, where a politician is expected to have some sort of grasp of and interest in a plethora of conflicting interests and issues. Even friends say that she appeared to regard the Senate as a nice club and as a reward for services rendered.

Charles Haughey sees Valerie as essentially a 'pragmatist in everything she did. She didn't have a philosophical view of politics. We didn't have conversations about politics in an abstract way. She was just committed to Fianna Fáil. She saw it as the party of reality. She decided she liked me and that was that. She wanted to be in the Senate for what she could do there. Power was a means to an end for her. She didn't want power for herself, but she did want to be where the action is so that she could influence things and get things done'. Valerie's other friend, Dr Tony O'Reilly, agrees with Mr Haughey's assessment of her pragmatism. 'She's got one very English trait. If you make a friend, as Churchill said, don't be just a fair-weather friend. Make the friendship apparent in times of foul sailing. She had a great belief in Charlie Haughey. She's not a woman to whom abstract nouns mean anything, so you would find it difficult to get a discussion with her on the nature of nationalism or the spiritual values of the monarchy. She sees the world in certain polarities. There is an upperclass and a working class and her mediation between these operates in a completely non-Socratic, non-analytical way. She sees the enemy forces and she wages battle.'

It was perhaps unfortunate that Valerie's arrival in the Senate coincided with the time when women's issues were climbing steadily up the political agenda. She was there because she was a woman, even if she didn't realise it, but she was unable to join in the intense cross-party debate and lobbying on social issues, such as contraception and the protection and safety of women within marriage. Here, perhaps, her background exerted a negative influence. 'I'm not a feminist. I find many feminists masculine. I like men to be men though I like them to behave as if I'm not a nitwit. But I like them to open doors. The feminine way of being is not to be tough. One has women's feelings, one can't behave as if one is a man when one is not. Women bring something different.' When Valerie does talk about women's issues it is always in the context of how things were in the 1920s in Britain. From that perspective she sees things as having greatly improved for women. She feels that it was not the suffragette movement that won the vote, but the part women played in the war. Her perspective on feminism is frozen in the image of the woman who threw herself under galloping horses during the Derby, or Sylvia Pankhurst chained to the House of Commons' gates.

With that vantage point, it is not difficult to understand why she failed to understand the point of view of the oppressed working-class mother who wanted contraceptives freely available, and laws to protect her from domestic violence, not to mention equality of job opportunity and pay. Eileen Cassidy, who was a member of the *ad hoc* committee on women's affairs in the late 1970s, says that the committee's advice was taken, and as a result they were able to influence the drafting of several bills. 'The only thing that impassioned Valerie was the clinic. She wasn't interested in women's affairs at all.' Another female colleague says that 'she was very nationalist on the North but not at all pluralist on the social agenda. She had no interest in divorce or contraception. Not even an interest in discussing them. Any views she did express were very conservative'.

Valerie is the first person to acknowledge her own pragmatism. When

Charles Haughey was making his political come-back she was happy to help his rehabilitation, and he in turn did a good fundraising job for the clinic. So it was hardly surprising that when the heave against Jack Lynch became irresistible, she pinned her colours to the mast. 'If I was nice I should have been with Jack, but if you're in politics you're not, and also if you really think about the person who is going to run the country – Jack was too nice. But I was always a friend. George Colley was a very nice man, but Charlie was a leader.' One of Lynch's supporters in the Senate remembers that 'she became very close to Haughey and it was known that she switched allegiance. I was very conscious of it when the 1979 leadership issue came up. We had no vote in the Senate, which was good and bad, but it did mean that we could discuss it more openly with each other. She made it clear very early on that she was a Haughey woman. She was very openly pro-Haughey. People around George Colley felt that she had turned.' Charles Haughey reciprocated the public nature of her support by always making a point of clapping her on the back whenever they would meet and asking 'How's Lady Val?'. According to another Lynch supporter, Valerie's changing sides wasn't important because she didn't have a vote, and by the late 1970s, the source points out, Lynch 'was a toughened politician and had been through a lot since 1966. He was unlikely to have been hurt by her lack of loyalty'.

Valerie's period in the Senate awakened her political ambitions, and for a while it looked as if she might join Charles Haughey in his northside constituency where, in the 1981 general election, on a last effective count basis, the party was 5 per cent short of the votes necessary to take three of the four seats there. In the end Basil's illness intervened, and instead of going on the hustings Valerie accompanied her husband to London for treatment for his cancer. Basil's illness and death coincided with an intense and traumatic period in Irish political life. There were three elections between June 1981 and November 1982. The first returned a Fine Gael/Labour coalition led by Garret Fitzgerald, while in February 1982 the second election brought Charles Haughey back as Taoiseach. Nine months later, however, at the height of an internal crisis within Fianna Fáil, Labour and Fine Gael once again coalesced and formed a government in December.

It was during this last election campaign that Valerie was asked to run for Fianna Fáil in Dun Laoghaire. This was the constituency of two of Mr Haughey's leading opponents, Dr Martin O'Donoghue and David Andrews, both of whom were members of the club of twenty-two which had initiated a heave against Haughey the previous February. Dun Laoghaire was a five-seater and was a vulnerable constituency for Fianna Fáil where, in 1981, a slight swing of 4 per cent away from the party could have reduced it to holding only one seat. Martin O'Donoghue hung on in the first election in 1982 and was a thousand votes ahead of Fine Gael's Monica Barnes when he took the seat on the last count.[6] Valerie told the *Evening Herald* that she had been telephoned by Fianna Fáil, while in Paris on business, and asked to return to seek selection at a convention in the constituency: 'I'm not a complete novice to politics of course. I have been in the Senate for many years and know about the legislature. I was very surprised when Fianna Fáil asked me to stand in the borough, but I was not imposed by the party leaders'.[7]

The Irish Times noted in its pre-election analysis that:

> Valerie Lady Goulding is the spanner in the works, so to speak. A great many voters in Dun Laoghaire will admire the work she has done at the Rehabilitation Institute (sic) and this will be reflected in the poll. She must surely attract votes from across the parties and if she is eliminated at the count, the dispersal of her votes could decide the contest between Dr O'Donoghue and Ms Barnes.

Writer Sam McAughtry went canvassing and found her 'immensely popular and clearly well known. People went out of their way to meet her, and to express their admiration for her work'.[8] On the basis of the canvas McAughtry thought that she was a sure bet. But whether Valerie was aware of it or not, there were strong political undercurrents in Dun Laoghaire, where the party was deeply split on the issue of the Haughey heave. Many cumann members sympathetic to Dr O'Donoghue, resented Valerie's presence, seeing her as a direct threat to his seat. At Fianna Fáil headquarters the stated aim of Valerie's inclusion on the ticket was to stop the decline in their percentage of the vote. *Magill* noted after the election that 'Fianna Fáil drafted in

Lady Valerie Goulding in a bid to stem their alarming decline. Martin O'Donoghue showed signs of actually feeling the darkening clouds as he tried to get out from his tangled relationship with the leader whose every word he distrusted.'[9]

With passions running high, many of those close to Dr O'Donoghue saw Charles Haughey's hand in the matter, arguing that he was prepared to risk the second seat if that meant punishing O'Donoghue for his part in the heave. According to this view of events, Mr Haughey was aware of the figures and knew that there were not two quotas for Fianna Fáil in Dun Laoghaire. He would, again according to this version of events, have known how David Andrews and Dr O'Donoghue managed the constituency between them in order to maximise their vote. In short, it was held by O'Donoghue loyalists that Valerie Goulding had been imposed on the constituency in order to get their man. Valerie denies in the most emphatic terms that this was the case, and she denies any knowledge of it. 'I was there to help keep up the vote. I was there to help keep Martin's seat. I never thought that I would get in and I told everyone that I'd be happy if I got a respectable vote. I remember saying to people that if I got two thousand votes I'd be happy.'

Valerie is adamant that she was not aware of any problem in Dun Laoghaire, but some of her friends and election helpers who came into the constituency during the campaign acknowledge that their presence was resented. Many of her friends feel that she was used, though they accept that she does not see it that way. Less sympathetic politicians find it hard to accept that Valerie did not understand the consequences of her inclusion on the ticket, and some ponder whether she might not have had a misguided view of her vote-winning ability. Valerie denies all this speculation, stating simply that she ran to 'help save the seat' for Fianna Fáil. In the end Dr O'Donoghue's first-preference vote dropped from 6944 to 4053 while Valerie polled 2492 first preferences. In all the Fianna Fáil vote dropped by 2.6 per cent while Fine Gael's jumped by about 4 per cent. Monica Barnes topped the poll and her party took three seats. Dr O'Donoghue lost his seat, while David Andrews retained his, as did Labour's Barry Desmond. As things turned out Fianna Fáil simply did not have enough votes to win two seats, with or without Valerie Goulding. Charles Haughey says that he was 'amazed that Valerie didn't poll better in Dun Laoghaire. But it's a funny place. She would have been better off in Clontarf – she's known there. It was the wrong constituency'. As to her performance on the hustings: 'she wasn't so great. Her accent and mannerisms were not of the popular sort. But it was a big thing for us to have her. It gave us credibility. It made some people think again about Fianna Fáil. If Valerie Goulding is in the party they can't be all that bad'.

Following Fianna Fáil's election victory in February 1987, Valerie announced her intention of running for the Senate. She was nominated by the board of the Central Remedial Clinic for the administrative panel. Once again she set herself the arduous task of trying to convince county councillors up and down the country that they should abandon tradition and close political ties and vote for an individual who had nothing to trade. She told the *Bray News* that she reckoned that 'there are three Fianna Fáil seats to be taken, but I am the fourth candidate on the ticket so it will be very difficult. However, if I can survive the early rounds of the count I hope to pick up transfers to see me through'.[10] Valerie polled badly, barely garnering a handful of votes and, much to the disappointment of her friend Geraldine Cruess-Callaghan, she was not included in Charley Haughey's choice of eleven nominees. Geraldine is a loyal and old friend of Valerie's, so it is no unkindness to say that her feelings closed her eyes to the realities of politics on this occasion.

Both Valerie and Geraldine worked for Mr Haughey's son, Seán, in his bid to take a Dáil seat in Dublin North East. Geraldine felt that Mr Haughey owed it to Valerie to nominate her when she failed to take a Senate seat. Geraldine is a determined lady, and when an opportunity arose to talk to the people who might be able to help Valerie get a seat, she seized it. 'When Haughey's mother died I took Valerie to the church. We sat in a side bench near the front. I thought it was important that she meet all the people she knew. I saw Brian Lenihan and I told her to talk to him and then we met Cardinal O'Fiaich who slipped into the church by a side entrance. Afterwards I was determined to write to Cardinal O'Fiaich to ask him to suggest to Charlie that he should nominate Valerie to the Senate. But I didn't get a reply. Two days before the announcement of the nominations I rang Armagh and spoke to the cardinal's secretary, who assured me that if I'd written a letter to the cardinal he would have seen it. I really did feel that she deserved the nomination. All kinds of people got it.' Charles Haughey reflects dispassionately on what might have been. '*Realpolitik* won the day in 1987. I couldn't say – "here's the seat because I like you". There were so many considerations, balances, all kind of factors.'

Looking back, Valerie does not regard her political experiences as her finest hour and yet one senses that she wants her political loyalty, at least, acknowledged. Charles Haughey describes her 'as an achiever and a doer with tremendous sincerity and integrity: a great feeling for the people. She wasn't just a do-gooder: she was do-gooder who was successful at it. She saw politics as part of her route to her achievement. But she couldn't have been a great politician. She wouldn't have been a great backbencher – she's too individualistic – she would have had to have been the boss'.

1 *Ireland in the Twentieth Century*, John A Murphy. *The Gill History of Ireland*, 11, p125.
2 *Ibid.*
3 *Ibid.* p126.
4 The word 'Taca' is derived from the Irish word for help or support. Taca was an organisation that provided financial and fundraising support to Fianna Fáil.
5 A Taoiseach's nominee and later TD speaking to the author.
6 *Magill Election 1982, Magill Book of Irish Politics, 1993.*
7 *Evening Herald* interview with Séamus Counihan, 15 November 1982.
8 *The Irish Times*, 12 November 1982.
9 *Magill Book of Irish Politics 1983*, p62.
10 *Bray News*, 13 March 1987.

9

UNCOMFORTABLE
TRANSITIONS

It is not in Valerie's nature to let go of things easily. Though she had supported the idea of employing a professional and younger managing director at the CRC, she found it difficult to step sideways and out of the limelight. Her successor as managing director, Ken Holden, understands how painful it was. 'It was her life: Valerie was the clinic.' She formally retired in August 1980 and perhaps would have been fulfilled enough by her activities in the Senate had Basil's death not intervened. After he became ill in early 1981, Valerie dropped everything, and when it was clear that he was not going to get better, she took no further part in the election campaign for the Senate. Although Valerie had resigned as managing director, she was still chairman of the board of governors until 1985, when she was replaced by her son Ham. Ken Holden felt that, initially at least, Valerie had 'let go to the extent of being content to be involved and informed, and to remain the public image of the clinic. I felt that she had adjusted to the change in her role'. Fellow board member Noel Judd explains, 'Valerie had strong views on how money should be raised. She felt that some people were not pulling their weight and she wanted younger governors on the board. She was very frustrated. Some of us disagreed with her because we felt that our need of money was not the same as in the early days. When we agreed to take part in the Rehab Lottery she took great exception because the CRC's name was not used.'

Ken found the relationship with Valerie less easy when, having given up her executive offices, she made her feelings felt on issues like the Rehab Lottery. 'We crossed swords on Rehab and on the United Way concept of planned donation to charity (where monies were deducted from salaries at source, by agreement). I believed that the old traditional fundraising was over. It's impossible to raise money from flag days. They can look like a visible success, but the bottom line is that not much money is achieved that way. Real money is pulled in by something like United Way, although it has not worked in Ireland. Valerie didn't like either method of raising money – she wanted to do it her way.' Valerie's views on the Rehab Lottery arrangements were so strong that it created a difficult situation for Ham who, as chairman, vehemently opposed her views. Because of this conflict Ham resigned. Geraldine Cruess-Callaghan understands what Valerie was trying to do in the later 1980s and shares her concern about how effective the Rehab Lottery was as a means of raising funds for the clinic. 'It's a young people's world; she wanted to get new blood onto the board of governors, and when Ham took over, the idea was that the older board members would go too. One or two did go, including me, but that was it. She resigned to give example but they didn't follow.'

Against the advice of many of her friends, Valerie expresses her difference of opinion about fundraising policy at the clinic to anyone who will listen. She is outraged by any suggestion that she is out of touch, and claims that she is far from old-fashioned when it comes to her ideas on how money should be raised. Valerie's hurt is very real, and the fact that she feels that her opinion and comment is not being listened to is a cause of great anguish to her. 'I'm all in favour of new methods – TV, radio etc. I got Saatchi and Saatchi in to do an ad, but they wouldn't use it. They think that I'm old-fashioned but it's the other way round.' Ken Holden feels that following Valerie's resignation as managing director, it might have helped the transition she was trying to make had a more structured way of including her in the life of the clinic been formulated. 'It concerned me at the time that she was so good at distancing herself from the clinic that we should have found a better way for her to channel her energies into the CRC.'

The clinic's former chief superintendent physiotherapist, Kay Keating, feels that Valerie's difficulties arose when, following her retirement, decisions were made that 'she wasn't involved with and when she wasn't involved with them she disagreed with them'. It is never easy to watch the chasm of age and experience come between oneself and one's child: the Central Remedial Clinic was Valerie's baby.

199

Oddly it is the only baby that she has not willed to walk alone. Her successor Ken Holden says that 'it would be a tragedy if people somehow glossed over her achievement. The clinic was more or less finished in her time. Can anyone imagine going out and creating that from scratch. The critics should stand back and say – "could I have done that?". If they are honest the answer is – absolutely not'.

The fact that Valerie found it difficult to let go of the reins is understandable. Anyone who so single-mindedly devoted their energy to one cause as she did, would tremble at the prospect of the void ahead. She is the first to say that she is not a baby lover. 'I told Ham when his children were born that I'd be no good with them until they were about six.' Given that view it was unlikely that Valerie would easily settle down into the role of the average Irish grandmother. Lingard points out that because of the overlap between his mother's social life and her work, almost her entire world revolved around the clinic. Geraldine Cruess-Callaghan feels that Valerie was 'so dedicated she didn't have time to make many friends. She had one goal all her life and it was hard when that was gone'.

Her need to 'do something' was evident in the months after Basil's death. She opened a restaurant in the conference centre that Basil had built over the Dargle river. Each night at about half past seven Valerie would prepare to greet the guests as they arrived for dinner. Lingard feels that his mother had an artificial lease of life after Basil died. 'She was very creative. I think she started the restaurant because she wanted to prove that she could run a business on her own. She wanted to prove it to herself.' Having got the restaurant off the ground, Valerie agreed to travel to Lebanon in January 1983 with John Bellingham, a member of the Order of Malta, in order to assess the services available to handicapped children there. During the visit she met Prince Lobkowicz, the Order's minister in Beirut. The prince agreed to Valerie's plan to try and build a remedial centre for a group called Sesobel (Service Social pour le bien être de l'enfant au Liban) who were caring for handicapped children in four centres in the eastern and northern suburbs of Beirut.

Sesobel was one of three groups that John Bellingham and Valerie felt it was possible to help – the other two being Mother Teresa's House of Peace for handicapped children and the Spastic Centre at Araya. The plan involved a promise from Valerie to raise fifty thousand pounds in Ireland which would be matched by the Order of Malta. It was also envisaged that a van would be purchased so that the children could be ferried to and from the new clinic. From what she learned on that trip Valerie thought that what was needed from Ireland was both physiotherapists and equipment. It was felt that Irish people would be more likely to contribute to the building of a clinic if young Irish volunteers were involved. On this basis it was agreed that a group of volunteers would make a return visit to Lebanon later in the year. According to John Bellingham's report, Valerie raised twenty-five thousand pounds, but was not put off, and decided to go ahead with her mission. She personally chose six members of the team who travelled out to Beirut in June:

> The first week of our stay in Lebanon was a bit of an anti-climax. The builders at Mar Elias had not yet made access to our quarters possible, and SESOBEL were not geared to integrate our group into their activities until the following week. Moreover the planning of our co-operation was the subject of long, verbose and repetitive meetings. The Irish group were impatient of all this and tempers became a bit frayed. Equally it must be said that the Lebanese felt that we were wanting them to change their plans to suit us, rather than our producing what they thought they most needed. This resulted in two of our group not working with SESOBEL, and preferring to concentrate themselves entirely to the House of Peace.[1]

Despite the many problems that her group faced, Valerie thinks that the seven-week trip was worthwhile. 'Just letting them see what was going on there is so important. They saw a lot of horrors, but seeing the rest of the world is so important for young people. Two of the group did say that they wanted to come home after the first few days, but we sorted it out in the end. Things move more slowly in Arab countries and they were so anxious to get in and help the children. I think they felt that we were being socialised with rather than helping. We hoped to contribute by advising on physiotherapy skills. But the success of that trip was undoubtedly that the group learned about somewhere they only heard about on television. I really liked the nuns at Mother

Teresa's place and I had promised that I would go back. So I travelled back again in August and got in on the last plane before the airport closed. It was terrible, I couldn't get up to the North to where the Christians were, and I couldn't get to Mother Teresa's. I was very disappointed when I did get back to the Muslim centre where we had worked in June; things were back to the old ways. We had hoped that the girls would have tried to use the skills we had taught them, but it was the same as before our group went in.'

> Lady Valerie Goulding, who was trapped in intensive shelling in Beirut this week, arrived safely last night at the UNIFIL headquarters in Naquora, southern Lebanon, after leaving the capital city by road with a UN convoy.
>
> 'It was a bit noisy for a few days', she said in a telephone interview last night, and added that she still hopes to organise a further Irish medical mission to Beirut to aid handicapped children there.
>
> 'I certainly would not bring anyone out at the moment', she said. 'But when things calm down, I see no reason why we shouldn't come back . . . . '
>
> She travelled to Beirut last Friday, hoping to see the Lebanese Health Minister and discuss an expansion of the work of the Irish relief mission. However, she said from Naquora last night that this meeting had not been possible as the ministries were all closed because of the heavy fighting.
>
> Despite rockets and shells exploding in the city, Lady Valerie travelled through several militia road-blocks and managed to visit two of the centres where the Irish mission worked and where, she said, the children were being well cared for.
>
> She saw many casualties of the fighting, and at one point on Wednesday night encountered a burning car with two victims inside, one dead and one so badly injured that there was nothing she could do to help.[2]

In the end Valerie was evacuated by Irish army personnel on the advice of the chargé d'affaires, Piarse Mac Anraoi. Lingard describes his mother's experiences as straight out of *Boy's Own*. 'There was an element of bravado in it. She had to be rescued by the Irish army, driven down to Jerusalem in order to get her out through Tel Aviv.' On a more serious note Ken Holden, who travelled out to meet the mission during its stay in Beirut, says that it was an 'ego trip. A single person cannot make a significant impact on a situation like Beirut. It didn't do any harm, but it didn't do any good either. I think that it was an attempt to recreate the past. There was no clear plan'.

Lady Goulding will be travelling to Jordan at the invitation of Prince Ra'ad in Amman to discuss the building of a clinic for the disabled along the lines of the Central Remedial Clinic, she announced privately yesterday.

Lady Goulding was attending her farewell ceremony in the Clontarf clinic as founder and chairwoman. She adds that she was bowing out of her restaurant – already sold with her Enniskerry home to Tony Ryan of Guinness Peat Aviation – and also had plans to go back to Beirut, which she visited a year ago.

'And I haven't lost sight of my political ambitions, either', said the tireless former senator. 'My ambitions are alive and well, and I've a good few years to go. I think I'm probably too old to make deputy, but I'd like to be senator again.'[3]

Valerie went to Jordan in February 1984 to assess a planned project to build a social and sports complex for the handicapped. 'I was invited out to talk about the clinic. King Hussein's number two, Prince Ra'ad, asked me to go out. They had a lot of problems with children suffering from burns because of the particular kind of oil lamps that they used in the desert.' The site for the complex had already been donated and one hundred and fifty thousand dollars had been collected locally. Prince Ra'ad was seeking EC funding under its European non-governmental organisation scheme. 'My job was to tell the architect and the interpreter where things should go and how it should be built.' Valerie wrote to Prince Ra'ad Ibn Zaid after her first look at their plans:

I am most interested in your project for a sports complex for the handicapped which will combine a day centre where all the handicapped can meet together. It is a very large undertaking and I should be most honoured to help your Royal Highness in any way possible. Perhaps we could have one more meeting to discuss what you would like us to do to help you to get the project underway as soon as possible. From what you have said to me, I believe you need, apart from the building, a Director of Activities together with a Sports Manager and occupational therapist who would come to Jordan for a period of time until somebody from your country can take over. The next item I think would be to endeavour to obtain financial assistance from the European Economic Community.

Valerie enjoyed the trip to Jordan, and although it was a short visit, she and Geraldine Cruess-Callaghan, who accompanied her, were taken to see Petra by their Jordanian hosts. Somewhere en route Valerie hurt her ankle and wasn't able to walk properly. But like many the Irish person before her she was lucky enough to run into an expatriate chef working in the hotel in Petra who on seeing that the famous 'Lady G' was in trouble, arranged for a jeep to carry her around the ancient city.

Valerie's next trip was to Ethiopia in late 1986. Looking back, she is unhappy about the visit because she feels that it was not a success. 'Cardinal O'Fiaich asked me to go out and assess the success of a number of small groups who were endeavouring to provide help and aid in the period after the big famine. Brenda Clarke came with me. We went all over the place in a jeep with Father Kevin Doheny who organises the Cheshire Homes in Africa. We stayed in Addis Ababa with the Sisters of Charity on the first night, and after that we went to see Mother Teresa's nuns at work in the city. We also visited a training centre for "street girls" run by nuns. Then we drove to Wallo Province where we saw a lot of Irish teams at work in all sorts of projects, including mother and baby clinics. We met Father Jack Finucane who told us about Concern's projects out there. We really did go everywhere. My main aim was to assess how the money that was being sent out was being spent. When we came back I formed a committee, and the idea was to have a big meeting to get the fundraising going. I had hoped to get some big names to come along but it didn't happen. Normally the newspapers were very good to me but when I said that there wouldn't be any big names at the meeting, they didn't cover it. This was the first time that I utterly failed. I didn't get the money that I'd promised for the people in Africa.'

During the 1980s Valerie was desperately seeking a new role. She had always liked to be 'at the centre of things' as Lingard points out and she wasn't used to playing a role off the centre stage. She was in the vanguard of an era when charity work and publicity became synonymous, and she strongly felt the urge to use her skills on new projects. She felt the frustration of a seasoned war-horse with no war to fight. Valerie has always acknowledged that her greatest skill was as a manipulator: she was second to none at getting people to do the things that she wanted them to do. She told Tim that it was her manipulative skills that got the clinic going. Dr Tony O'Reilly does not agree that Valerie is a manipulator. 'She's not a manipulator in the sense that that kind of person has forethought. Valerie is fundamentally encouraged in life by clear objectives and goals. She has almost a military mind. She looks and says not "why?" – but "why not?". She goes for it. She's not a manipulator – everybody knows her objective. She sees the objective – identifies the enemy. The enemy is apathy and indolence and an uncaring world and she enlists you in the troops. It's not subtle, you know what you are marching towards. She's unambiguous.'

Given her need to 'do something', to be active and to play a role, it was with great difficulty that she dealt with worsening and debilitating health problems. The clinic and her constant activism was perhaps Valerie's main source of emotional succour. Ham feels that, through the clinic, his mother was able to give vent to an emotional expression which she found difficult in her private relations. Dr O'Reilly understands Valerie's dilemma. 'You've got to equip yourself in life for the different time zones – for the ages of man with its different appetites and skills. You can't run the hundred yards when you're fifty-six or fifty-seven, but then there's lots of things that you can't do at eighteen that you can do at seventy-four. But Valerie had a unique focus and she unselfishly did not prepare herself for the time zones. So a certain loneliness set in, and in that sense she now feels that there should still be some great objective in her life.'

Reflecting on her work for the clinic, Valerie says that it is impossible to remember all of the children who passed through over the years. 'Billy Sugrue stands out. I remember bringing him to Boyd Dunlop back in the 1950s. He'd had rather a bad time of it. He came to us when he was two and everyone worked with him. I remember him as a floppy doll. Billy would do anything for me – he would walk for me. I hope he knows the encouragement that he is to people who see him working in the clinic now – a married man with two children. The other boy I'll never forget is Christy Nolan. He caught my imagination. There he was – a boy who couldn't move at all – yet his lovely blue eyes were so bright. He'd endeavour to smile and then an arm or leg would shoot out and he'd be embarrassed. I'd say to him – "Look, everyone's the same". There was something about him – it was his determination that got me. He was such a lovely boy with such courage. But he wasn't the only one with courage.'

Christopher expressed his feeling for Valerie in a poem he wrote when he was fourteen years of age. It was included in his first book, *Dam-Burst of Dreams*:

> Slowly, slowly, slowly,
> Love wishes as love does;
> Pealing bragging bells of faith
> In the sobbing place of woe,
> Fostering, lovely hope, asleep,
> Offended, and heart-worn,
> Giving measle-spotted help
> To a handicap man forlorn.
> Castigating gospel stories
> Of Samaritan special help,
> She diligently sought an answer,
> Kathleen found time, told well;
> Capitalizing on caring people
> Offering monetary help, 'twixt
> Love and serene suffering,
> They built a bridge to health;
> Now, celestial glory 'waits them,
> Graciously foretold, by One who
> Raised the crippled man Divinely,
> In Capernaum – so long ago.

A version of a life is just that: it is a view down the microscope of other people's love, jealousy and even hate. What is real or true is particular to he who tells the tale. One image that remains of all the stories, versions and legends of Valerie's life comes from Annie Goulding. 'Sometime, probably not long after we moved in, Valerie came down to stay with us in Allihies. We didn't have a lot of room and she decided to pitch her tent outside the house. We tiptoed out at about ten o'clock because we didn't want to disturb her. But there she was whistling in the tent just like a real girl guide keeping her spirits up.'

---

1 Report on the Order of Malta's Irish mission to the handicapped children of Lebanon, summer 1983, under the leadership of Lady Goulding, p8.
2 *The Irish Times*, 2 September 1983.
3 *The Irish Times*, 28 June 1985.